A NEWCASTLE BOYHOOD

1898–1914

1: The author photographed on February 20th, 1912, a few weeks before his fourteenth birthday. He is wearing a new suit, ready to go to Rutherford College (see chapter 13).

A NEWCASTLE BOYHOOD 1898-1914

FORTITER DEFENDIT TRIUMPHANS

Basil Peacock

Published jointly by Newcastle uponTyne City Libraries
and London Borough of Sutton Libraries & Arts Services

ILLUSTRATION ACKNOWLEDGEMENTS

1–11 and portrait photographs on cover: The author
12–31 and non-portrait photographs on cover: Newcastle upon
Tyne City Libraries.

First Published 1986

London Borough of Sutton Libraries and Arts Services
Central Library, St Nicholas Way, Sutton, Surrey.
Tel. 01-661 5050
© Text: Basil Peacock

ISBN 0–907335–16–0

Design: Shirley Edwards

Printed and bound in Great Britain
by Anchor Brendon Ltd, Tiptree, Essex

CONTENTS

Foreword

In a previous book of mine, an autobiography entitled "Tinker's Mufti, Memoirs of a Part-time Soldier" there is a short account of my early life when an infant and a schoolboy in Newcastle upon Tyne before the First World War. To my surprise, many readers declared it a most intriguing chapter in the volume, and asked for more details. An eminent, widely-read lady journalist, many years younger than myself, who had read the text in manuscript, suggested I should extend it to book length, describing in detail the mode of life and my generation of the Peacock family, all members of which were born in the nineteenth century. She added poignantly "You, Basil, being the youngest, and one of the latest-born Victorians should do so, because within a few years there will be no-one left alive who could describe family life in the late nineteenth and early twentieth century from personal experience."

I was a little startled at this remark as I had not realised till then that those persons born in the reign of Queen Victoria were becoming a little sparse, and those must all be very senior citizens, mostly octogenarians or even older. I had looked upon my circle of menfriends, all seemingly elderly, as belonging to my genration, till I became aware that few of them could recall incidents before 1914, being then only babes or unborn.

So, while memory serves I have set down in the following pages recollections, and the history of my lower middle-class family, their surroundings, trials, diversions and thoughts, before modernity, new inventions and social changes brought about by the First World War, altered then completely. It is written for the dwindling number of my contemporaries and the growing number of persons, living in this frenetic world who are curious to learn about a different way of life and conduct in days that are gone nearly a century ago. Students of social history have probably read historians' accounts of those days, but my recollections of living in them may amuse and add to their knowledge.

CHAPTER ONE

Home of my Childhood

In 1905, when aged seven, I left the house where I was born and did not see it again until I was an octogenarian, and then only by chance.

My brother Jim, several years older than myself, had asked me to deliver a lecture on "Soldiers and Soldiering in Ancient Times" to a Society of Senior Male Citizens who met in a hall in Heaton Road attached to Heaton Presbyterian Church, Newcastle upon Tyne. During a tea interval half way through my discourse, I suddenly realised I had been in that hall before and stood on the same platform facing an audience of Sunday School children, and attempting to recite some infantile verses of doggerel for their entertainment. I recalled with embarrassment that I was suddenly struck with acute stage fright, dried up, and ended in tears. Hoping that none of my present audience remembered the incident which happened over seventy years ago when some of these elderly men had attended Sunday School in the same church hall, I finished my lecture. It was received with generous applause, and no-one mentioned my first appearance on that stage.

Replying to some kind words from listeners, I found myself using dialect and local expressions which I had not done during many years of absence from my native town, and began to feel some nostalgia, a common emotion in all Northumbrians exiled from their birth place. The feeling was intensified when my brother and I emerged from the church, and I sniffed the brisk North Country air, as the sense of smell evokes remembrances more acutely than other senses. Looking half-right across the road, I caught sight of a name plate on a wall reading "CHELTENHAM TERRACE", and I exclaimed to brother Jim "We used to live there in Number Nineteen – is the house still standing?"

"Yes," he replied, "though I have never entered it since we lived there."

Full of curiosity and sentiment, I said "Come, let us view it and maybe see inside."

Jim was not so enthusiastic, being a little shy, but agreed when I quoted "I may not pass this way again."

The terrace seemed little changed except that the entrance to it had been barred for motor traffic. It consisted of about thirty close-built houses on each side of a road, the original surface of which was made of granite sets. Number Nineteen stood well and firm, looking fresher than I remembered it, which was surprising as it had been built nearly one hundred years before, and looked as though it would stand for another century. The thick sandstone surrounds to doors and windows had been scrubbed to remove the grime of decades and given a light-coloured coating, and the woodwork brightly painted. In our period of residence, most outside and inside paintwork was a dull yellow or brown because light colours would soon tarnish in the dust and smoke of Newcastle, a sooty industrial town.

Each house in the terrace had a miniature garden about four feet wide in front of it, showing signs of care and cultivation. In our time they were mainly scratch places for cats and dogs, as the soot and even coal dust in the atmosphere precluded successful gardening. Those householders who managed to grow some privet or tatty chrysanthemums were counted as skilled horticulturists, making use of the horse manure gathered from the street. There were three front steps to each dwelling, leading to a small tiled level surface before the front door. These and the gardens raised the tone of the terrace, as in many streets in Newcastle there was only one front step from the pavement to inside the house.

Diffidently I rang the electric bell which had been fitted to the front of Number Nineteen, wondering what our reception would be if any one answered the door. A youngish-looking lady opened it, and before she could ask our business I raised my hat, handed her my professional card on which I was shown as an author, and said "Madam, we sincerely apologise for this unexpected visit, but my brother and I lived in this house many years ago, and I was born in it, so you may understand our interest."

She read my card, looked us over keenly and evidently decided that we were not two geriatric gangsters "casing a joint", but two mild, harmless, old gentlemen, perhaps a little gaga, and said "You were born in this house?"

2

"Yes," I replied, "in 1898."

"Then," she continued with a smile, "I know you would like to see inside again", and with usual North Country custom added: "I'm sure you would like a cup of tea."

We thanked her, but declined her offer of tea, saying our visit must be brief as I had to catch a train back to my home in London.

Behind the solid-timbered front door was another, half glass, and the kind hostess ushered us through this into what she called "the hall" which we had always referred to as the downstairs passage. Unexpectedly, it looked larger and less cramped than I remembered it from childhood, probably because it was close carpeted, our massive hall-stand had gone, there were no bicycles leaning against the walls, and the decorations were light and cheerful. If it was unlit after dark when I was an infant I was a little timid of venturing in it, thinking that odd things like goblins lived there.

Our house was termed a left-handed one, which meant that the main downstairs rooms were to the left of the passage. For some unfathomable reason, my sisters declared a left-handed home was a little superior to a right-handed one and luckier.

Our hostess showed us into her lounge, which we had always referred to as "the front room", and, on special occasions "the parlour". It was furnished and decorated in modern style so it was light and airy – so different from the room we remembered. Then, it was furnished in crowded Victorian style and similar to most lower middle-class parlours when furniture and fittings were made to last a lifetime.

The chairs, tables, whatnots, etc., must have been made before 1870 and acquired by my parents soon after. The woodwork was all dark walnut, and the upholstery was shiny black hair-cloth supported by springs and horse-hair padding. The actual seats were very rounded and smooth, so that lightweight users, especially children, glided off them onto the floor. There was another rather painful hazard when stout strands of horse-hair, escaping from the padding, shot up through the cover and pierced the bottom of the sitter. This happened more frequently to male users, because the number of underclothes worn by ladies in those days afforded some protection.

The principal items were a large, heavy "grandfather's" chair and a "grandmother's" type, the latter so wide that it must have been made to be used by ladies wearing crinolines or bustles. I recall finding a strange-looking small cushion in my mother's bedroom and being informed in a whisper by my eldest sister that it was called a bustle, but not told its use. We had a large sofa against the wall of the parlour. It had one raised curly end, and a large cylindrical bolster with a tassel hanging from one end, on which I was occasionally allowed to sit astride on the floor, pretending it to be a horse. There were home-knitted wool antimacassars on chair backs which provided some colour to the room and at the same time protected the upholstery from hair oil, which most males used profusely in those days. The main oval table in the middle of the room was draped with a large cloth reaching almost to the floor to hide the legs; as legs were counted as rather indelicate appendages in those times, and even wooden ones were sometimes covered in cotton pantaloons.

There were several smaller tables scattered about, useless for sitting at, being either too high or too low. One had an octagonal-shaped top with scalloped edges, and was placed in the bow window, supporting a large aspidistra plant in an ornate pot.

The focal point in our parlour was the fireplace, with its brass fender and fire-irons, and broad mantelpiece draped in thick tapestry with a bobble fringe. On it stood three objects which fascinated and delighted me when a child. The most prized possession in our home stood in the middle – an immense ornamental heavily-gilded clock under a huge glass dome. It was about twenty-four inches in height, and represented a Chinese peasant pushing a large singled-wheeled barrow filled with fruit and vegetables. The dial was set into the side of the barrow, made of porcelain with gold minute and hour hands. After visiting China later in life, I now realise that the maker had never seen a Chinaman nor a Chinese hand-cart, but could be congratulated on his exotic idea of them. It is now a valuable piece of Victoriana in the possession of my niece, and still faithfully recording the correct time.

The clock used to be flanked by two large lustres consisting of many glass prisms dangling from porcelain supports which produced all the colours of a rainbow when light fell on them, and tinkled when they moved. These, too, would be valuable pieces of Victoriana if they had not been given away as rubbish when the family modernised their second home.

4

2 (*left*): The author's mother, Jane Briggs, as a young woman, around the time of her marriage. She was usually known as Jenny.   3 (*right*): The author's parents, James and Jane Peacock, on their wedding day, c. 1880.

Except for these items, our front room was a gloomy room even though it faced south. This was because of the window furnishings. There were heavy Venetian blinds made of wooden slats and were rarely drawn right up to the top of the windows. Over these were substantial lace curtains which prevented passers-by looking into the room, and also light coming in. Finally, heavy velvet curtains hung from wooden rings on a stout curtain rod, which were closed at night to retain heat from the fire in the room.

Brother Jim and I complimented our hostess on her bright lounge, and she was amused when we briefly described the former appearance of the room. She conducted us to her dining-room, which we used to call our back or sitting-room, because in the old days people of our class never dined, but just had our meals, usually in the kitchen except on Sundays. I could remember little of that part of the house except that the windows looked out on our backyard, and there used to be a very large table on which we played ping-pong with long-handled racquets made like double-sided tambourines.

We asked to see the kitchen, as so much of our early lives was spent there, so our guide took us along the passage, and Jim nudged me, saying, "Mind the step", reminding me that the floor of the back quarters of the house was about nine inches lower than the front. There was a step down just beneath the kitchen door, a continual hazard to members of the family who forgot it was there, even after long residence. We were a little disappointed that the cast-iron coal fireplace with its oven and hot-water boiler had been replaced by modern kitchen fittings, because it used to be the power plant of the whole house for cooking and warmth. It was a very welcoming piece of equipment, with its blazing fire, a singing kettle on a trivet, and shining steel fender. It also provided a great deal of hard work for the females of the family, who blackleaded all the dull metal twice a week and polished up the shiny parts with emery paper.

I was particularly pleased that what we used to call "Mother's cupboard", built under the stairs, was still there with its original door and old-fashioned sneck (local word for latch), because it delighted me when an infant; a sort of private playroom and hiding-place full of intriguing smells and curious objects stored in it. I could operate that sneck long before I could turn a door handle.

6

Jim and I were permitted to peep into the scullery behind the kitchen, but naturally the old enormous stone washing-up sink and gigantic clothes mangle had gone and been replaced by modern equipment. We thought it injudicious to ask to see the upper floor of the house, but as we were thanking and saying farewell to our hostess in the passage, I glanced up the stairs and was amazed to note that the enormous frosted glass screen was still in situ on the half landing. Through a door in it, one gained access to the bathroom and toilet thus providing extra privacy for users. I think this was called a modesty screen by builders, and as it was still standing they built well in those distant days nearly a century ago.

Brother Jim and I left 19 Cheltenham Terrace, speaking sentimentally of the time we had lived in it, and then sadly, knowing that we were the only surviving members of the family of eight whose home it was in Victorian and Edwardian times.

CHAPTER TWO

A Muster of Peacocks

At the end of the nineteenth century, our family consisted of father, mother and six children: three boys and three girls. There might have been four boys, but the earliest-born died in babyhood. When the family took up residence in Cheltenham Terrace, there were only five children, and it was thought that the progeny was complete, so my advent in 1898 was something of a surprise to many of my relatives, who probably thought there were enough in this muster of Peacocks.

The medieval term for a group of peacocks was an ostentation or a pride, and most authorities on derivation of surnames agree that "Peacock" originated as a descriptive nickname for a man given to more flamboyance in dress and manner than his neighbours. As common folk had only one name, that given to them at their christening, the nickname was probably only applied to their *seigneur*, and later adopted by vassals as a surname, and in some cases by the local inn-keeper as a sign for his house.

Now, the study of genealogy is becoming a popular pastime, and when gathering material for this book I tried to discover if our family could claim any kinship with notable persons named Peacock listed in national biographic dictionaries. It would have been pleasant to discover any connection, however faint, with the gentleman named Peacock, Lord Mayor of London in 1532, the ancient family of Peacocks in County Durham whose coat of arms displays three gold peacocks on a black shield, or Thomas Love Peacock, the writer and poet; but I had to conclude that our forefathers were very ordinary folk – part of the "commonalty" – to quote my father who was addicted to using this expression. No doubt our clan have been Novocastrians or Tynesiders for at least two centuries, and none of them have attained riches or were desperately poor, though frequently impecunious.

My mother was Jane Briggs – a very typical Tynesider who like many persons in North East England showed traces of Scandinavian and Friesland ancestry, because people from Northern Europe invaded and settled in Northumberland and Durham during the decline of Roman rule in Britain. She was short in stature, but immensely strong and active till late in life; she needed to be, looking after her large family, after giving birth to seven children over a period of fourteen years, and during that time assisting father in his business. She had the typical greyish-blue keen eyes common to Northumbrians, the colour of the North Sea. My brother once met a Danish lady in a tramcar in Copenhagen and declared she could be the twin sister of our mother.

She came from a family of deep-sea and inshore sailors, and her father and our Uncle Jack Briggs were master keelmen on the River Tyne, and part owners of a small tug. Keels is the term used on Tyneside for wherries, barges and small craft. One of the first songs I learnt when an infant was "Weel May the Keel Row". Working keels for transferring cargo was a profitable business in the nineteenth century, and the Briggs family was counted reasonably prosperous, as they lived near the river in a place called Quality Row which was a cut above the surrounding streets.

Mother received elementary education at a church school founded by Methodists, fitting for girls of her social class. The curriculum consisted of instruction in the three "R's" plus sewing, needlework, and orthodox Protestantism, counted sufficient for future mothers of families. In those times, there were few situations for middle-class females in trade or professions, and marriage was their hopeful future. However, when she left school in her early teens, she worked for a time in a milliners' shop and learned some dressmaking; a useful accomplishment, because later in life she had to spend much time altering her children's clothes when they grew out of them and fitting the garments to younger offspring. I remember being clothed in one of my eldest brother's suits, cut down to half-size to fit me, as a school outfit, and my embarrassment when wearing it.

She cared for and cherished her children: "did her duty by them" as friends and acquaintances remarked, but I feel the boys received more attention than the girls – usual in most families. She averred she had no favourites, but she had, and was always so busy with household and other duties that she had little time for petting and endearments. I cannot recall any of us being addressed as "darling" or "dearest", or by playful nicknames, and neither can I recall many endearments used in other families of the Peacock clan. Though Northumbrians are usually deeply sentimental folk, they often cover their kindly feelings with rough words, not wishing to be thought prim, or "a softie". However, there is one word of endearment in frequent use – "canny" – which in Northumbrian dialect means attractive and lovable, so that a sweet child is addressed as a "canny bairn"; a pleasant woman as a "canny hinny"; a kindly man as a "canny chap or bugger"; this last doubtful word need have no lewd meaning in the North East.

Mother could be a tartar, if vexed or worried, and could be very sharp with us, but I never knew her to slap anyone – her words were enough. Her favourite oaths were "what the dickens", and "by the living Harry", a very old expression referring to Henry the Eighth, or to Harry Hotspur of Northumberland, but I doubt if she was aware of this.

I have a photograph taken before her marriage which shows her as a comely little lady, and I have reason to believe that she was a lively lass, with several beaux, before taking up with my father.

In contrast to my mother, my father was above medium height, with a lean physique, and never ran to fat or even a paunch. He had the build of a runner, and in his youth won many prizes at amateur athletic meetings in sprint, quarter- and half-mile races. His facial expression was always that of a kindly, sensitive man, and I never saw him without a beard, always neatly trimmed to a point akin to that of General Smuts. As he also had a similar figure, he was once mistaken for that eminent soldier who was visiting Armstrong College, now the University, in Newcastle after the First World War.

My father was born in 1858 in Lambton Place, Newcastle. His father was a skilled artisan, and worked in one of the large engineering works on the Tyne. He had some education, which enabled him to become a spokesman for his fellow-workers when dealing with the bosses, and suffered for it because this was the period when trade unions were hardly recognised as bargaining organisations. Like most leaders of working men, in those early days, my grandfather was a deeply religious man, but became unpopular with his employers and had to take up another trade as a wood-turner. My father inherited some of his characteristics, and was always prepared to stand up for justice or to express an unpopular opinion if convinced in his own mind.

10

In the middle of the last century, there were few, if any, state schools, and most elementary education for the lower classes, if they received any at all, was provided by charitable organisations or churches of various denominations; so the majority of the working class were illiterate. Fortunately for my father, his parents paid for him to receive elementary education at what was termed a Dame School; fees two or three pence per week. Dame Schools were private, usually conducted by impoverished gentle-ladies in their own homes, where instruction in conduct, manners etc. were taught in addition to the three "R's". Father was an apt scholar who loved learning for its own sake as well as the advantages it brought. His education might have ended at the age of ten on leaving the Dame School, but due to a benefactor, a member of the church he attended, he received a place in a Mission School conducted in Blackfriars, which was part of an old monastery. This building still exists and has been renovated. Father must have been an outstanding scholar, because at the age of thirteen he became a sort of unpaid pupil teacher instructing the junior classes. Soon after this, his formal education ended, but for the remainder of his life he took every opportunity to acquire knowledge, especially of classical literature. By the time he was middle-aged, few persons outside universities knew more of the works of English poets, Shakespeare, and other great writers. It was most unfortunate that due to poverty in early life he had no opportunity to receive secondary education at a grammar school, because there is little doubt he would have obtained scholarships enabling him to go on to a university, and perhaps become a professor. However, by denying himself many luxuries, and even some necessities, he put four of his children through university, with some help from the state, and had the satisfaction of seeing one son become an eminent professor, and Fellow of the Royal Society, and two grandsons deans of university colleges.

On leaving school at the age of fourteen, he became a barrow-boy at a grocer's shop in the covered market in Newcastle, one of the first large markets to be built and which still exists, little changed. Later he opened a small shop in a newly-built suburb just outside the city walls, and I believe he found the capital to do so from a dowry my mother received on her marriage.

A few years later, after Mother had produced three children, he moved his business and his family to Byker, then a developing

4: The author's paternal grandfather, Aleck, with the first three children of James and Jane Peacock. Left to right: Alex, Edith, Jim.

5: The back of the previous photograph: a piece of late Victorian commercial design redolent of its period.

village east of the city across the Ouseburn which still flows in a deep valley dividing old Newcastle from the suburbs and Tyneside towns.

By the time the family had moved to Shields Road, a road bridge spanned the Ouseburn Valley and there were horse-trams using it, so Father must have thought he had picked a busy, quickly-developing area, likely to become a prosperous one. The family lived above the shop which provided nothing more than a modest living. My brothers who lived there told me that cows and goats grazed within a few yards of the back of the premises and most of the customers coming to the shop were poor working-class people who lived in the steep streets running down to the river, which even then were developing into slums.

After some years scraping a living, Father moved his business to a larger shop in Shields Road, nearer to the growing and more genteel suburb of Heaton which was sprouting like a mushroom from a small country village with a railway station. In those days, about nine decades ago, there were plenty of homes to let, so after a short residence in a small house bordering the railway, the ever-growing family moved to 19 Cheltenham Terrace, which counted as a step up in the world.

Father's shops never prospered, probably owing to lack of capital, and he was a man of such integrity that he always disdained sharp practice in business. He should never have been in business for himself, but he was so proud to be "his own master" that he never accepted any offers of situations in larger concerns, which would have provided a steady income greater than that he made from his own shops. Though there was often talk of imminent bankruptcy in our home, which frightened me when a child though I hardly knew what the word meant, this never happened, and he continued in business until the age of seventy, surviving by miracles during frequent periods of recession in trading. My elder brother once remarked: "The trouble with Father's shop was that like a badly handicapped race-horse – carrying too much weight – the profit was adequate to support a small family, but not one of six children".

After Father had given up business, I mentioned my childhood fears of the dread word "bankruptcy" to my mother. To my surprise she replied: "It would have been difficult to make him bankrupt, because I was always his greatest creditor as my dowry was always just on loan to him."

After retirement, Father devoted himself to classical study, and eventually wrote a long book about Shakespeare and his works. In it he set down all facts about the Bard discovered by other researchers, and précised the story and action of every play. He also wrote a lengthy chapter on the Baconian theory which attempts to prove that the learned man, Francis Bacon, wrote the works attributed to Shakespeare. If anyone deliberately or teasingly suggested that Bacon or anyone else was the author of the folios, Father became very heated, extremely annoyed, and fixing the doubter with piercing eyes would deliver a diatribe an hour or more in length to prove the Bard existed. The doubter usually cried "Enough", and fled the house before Father had finished.

He entitled his book "Shakespeare the Man and His Plays: a Book for the Commonalty". Though he had little formal education, Father had written a scholarly book after much study and extensive reading. It deserves to be published, but never was printed; but I possess a typescript professionally bound in hard-back. This, together with a silver cup he won when an athlete, are substantial mementoes I have of my worthy gentle parent. Like most of his generation he believed in self-help, too proud to accept anything he had not earned. He was in his late seventies before he could be induced to apply for an old age pension (Lloyd George's dole) though he had been entitled to one years before. He never possessed more than a trifle of capital in money, but to quote an old friend: "His capital was in his family".

Before the nineteenth century ended, my parents had begot six children, three boys and three girls. Their names, in order of seniority were: Alexander David; James Archibald; Edith Annie; Eleanor Briggs; Jennie Margaret; and Basil (myself). With the exception of the last, all these had been the baptismal names of former members of the very fecund Peacock and Briggs clans. Reflecting on the past, I can recall forty cousins of mine, but may have forgotten others. Not one of them was called Basil; and, because my brothers and sisters each had two, perhaps my parents were running out of ancestral Christian names, and had to give some thought to deciding on one for their last born. Later in life, my eldest brother told me that I was named after a character called Basil in *The Captain* magazine for boys, adding significantly:

"He was Greek and probably a brigand." My baptismal name was a trial to me most of my early life, being almost unknown in rough, industrial Newcastle, and thought somewhat cissy. If I had known that Basil means "Kingly", it would have embarrassed me even more, as a less kingly person than myself would be hard to find.

My eldest brother, Alexander, called after Father's father, was always referred to as Alec, and it was many years before I became aware of his full name. According to Mother, he had been a fractious and rumbustious infant – a "young limb" (of Satan), but showed intelligence and precocity at a very early age, in contrast to the younger children. He had many talents; learning came easy to him, and all his life he absorbed knowledge as a sponge does liquid. He did so well at school that he was frequently referred to by teachers, and our friends, when speaking to the other children, as "your clever brother", which did nothing for our self-esteem. However, I still regarded him as such until his death, just before his ninetieth birthday, with no trace of senility. He had been a professor at St. Andrew's and Dundee Universities, and an entomologist with a world-wide reputation.

The next in seniority – James Archibald – always brother Jim to me, was a gentle, placid individual, a good Christian, and a very "present help in times of trouble". His achievements in life were due to steady perseverance and tenacity, but his retiring and modest disposition precluded him from receiving recognition and rewards which he merited. He inherited his short but tough physique from Mother, and at the age of ninety was still a fit and active man.

My eldest sister, Edith Annie, next in line, was named after Father's deceased sister who died in a decline when a young adult, as so many did in those days. She had been much beloved, and my sister was similar in features and also well beloved. She was a born mother, though she never became one. She mothered the rest of the children, caring for others rather than herself, and like the willing horse did more than her fair share of duties in the house and in Father's business. She was a simple soul, never complaining of her lot in life, and was the most unselfish member of the family, taking the tenets of religion and the Church very seriously. She would have made an excellent nursing sister, and always wished to enter the nursing profession, but unfortunately for her she was so useful about the house and in business that she could not be spared to do so, and possibly my parents thought nursing a somewhat indelicate occupation. Tending to anyone ill or injured gave her much pleasure, and she dosed other members of the family with strange nostrums, mainly herbal, which she had learned about from unofficial medical articles in magazines. Later in life, I worked in hospitals, and realised that my parents had made a great mistake in preventing such a dedicated girl entering the healing profession.

After Edith came Eleanor – too soon she used to declare, as Mother had two babies to care for at the same time. Eleanor never had the robust constitution of the other children, but she survived her sisters. She was referred to as "our Nelly", a name she hated, and after some years pronounced that she must be addressed as Helen, a more refined title. She had the face and slender figure of present-day fashion models, but unhappily in the early decades of this century referred to as "a bit skinny". Sadly too, her reddish blonde hair, looked upon as very beautiful nowadays, was unkindly referred to as ginger. She yearned for the life depicted in the novelettes to which she was addicted, and she became a librarian.

My youngest sister, Jennie, took after Mother, with similar face and sturdy figure. She had a round, baby face all her life, was a little timid of those in authority, but bossed other children of her own age and younger, and eventually became a first-class infants' school teacher. She was curiously shy of the men, and I think, from a remark she made, was afraid of marriage and leaving home; refusing to respond to any young fellows who came with the intention of courting.

Though all my sisters would have made admirable wives, only Eleanor married, and then late in life. The longer I live, the sadder I feel that they did not find husbands, because they belonged to that generation of which a million men were killed early in life during the First World War, condemning almost a similar number of women to lifelong spinsterhood, with only memories of lads who came a-courting but fell in battle before they had time to wed.

After the birth of five children in rather quick succession, there was an interregnum until a stork dropped me down the chimney of 19 Cheltenham Terrace. I say "a stork" because the process of natural birth or sex was never mentioned in our family till we were all middle-aged. As children, when discussing the advent of babies,

17

6: The Peacock family in 1899. Left to right: Alex, Mrs Peacock, Basil, Jennie, Jim, Eleanor, James Peacock, Edith.

we inclined to Fairies, Stork, and Gooseberry Bush theories, but I remember my first girlfriend aged six told me in confidence that the postman brought them in his bag and delivered them to families who wanted them.

I was born on 2nd April, 1898, thus under the sign of the Zodiac, Aries. Astrologers declare that those born under this sign are destined in life for struggle, hardship, soldiering and war; and in my case, after I became a teenager, the forecast turned out curiously correct during forty-odd years.

During infancy and as a schoolboy, I seemed a very unlikely child to have a future that was to include much soldiering and hardship, because I was a rather tearful and timorous soul, cossetted as the baby of the family.

However, early in life I became a voracious reader, especially of adventure stories, once I had advanced beyond the "Tiny Tots" sort of publications. Children's comics were proscribed in our household, though I read them in secret if I obtained copies; with the result that I was introduced to better literature, such as stories and serials written by first-rate authors in the famous *Boys' Own Paper*, when younger than most of its readers. I read works of Henty, Beresford and Talbot Baines Reed when other children of my age were reading fairy stories, and remember reading early "Tales of the Outposts" in *Blackwood's magazine*, never dreaming that late in life I should write similar tales for that renowned pristine publication. I read so much that my eldest brother Alec declared I was a bookworm before I understood the meaning of the word. He said, "You should be out exploring, playing cricket or football with other lads, if you like adventures, go out and seek them – that is the meaning of the word – 'venture to', they will not come by sitting at home." A few years later I realised how right he was.

In the previous paragraphs I have endeavoured to present the individual characteristics of members of our Victorian family. I was fortunate to be born into it, because despite occasional tiffs and squabbles, it has remained close-knit and free from any of the deep quarrels which produce schism in many families. We were not a demonstrative lot: kissing, except after long separation, was rare; and loving words even more rare, but always there was deep lasting affection.

Unfortunately, I never knew any of my grandparents, as the

longest lived, my father's father, who lived with my family for some years, died before I was born. However, when preparing this book I gathered some facts about my forbears from my brothers, who had known some of them.

Some interesting documents came to light, and old letters written early in the nineteenth century which refer to members of the Peacock clan who were born in the early days of that century, before the Battle of Waterloo. There were some curious characters, and I have recorded something of their lives in the appendix of this book.

CHAPTER THREE

The Daily Routines

When I was just a lad, I thought that the days of the week were coloured, and even now associate them with various hues matching routine daily activities. Until I learned better, I thought that Monday was the first day of the week; and its colour was a dirty white. Tuesday was a greyish blue, Wednesday orange, Thursday similar to Tuesday but with a lighter tint, Friday was dull silver, Saturday a pleasant off-white, and Sunday red.

I also associated them with the main course of mid-day dinners, because if I remembered the day of the week I could guess the type of food which would be placed on the table. The weekly menus hardly varied throughout the years. I could also guess the household tasks which would be undertaken each day by Mother and my sisters; the male members of the family rarely, if ever, took any part in these activities or were expected to, being what are now termed "male chauvinist pigs".

In those days, the washing and laundering of clothes, table-linen and bed-linen, dominated most family routines, because there were no washing-machines and detergents which now make the task easy.

Monday was the starting day, and when the family was breakfasting a woman helper arrived wearing a man's cloth cap secured to her hair with a large hat pin. This was *de rigueur* for washerwomen, who usually had large families of their own, but needed a few shillings to add to the husband's earnings by doing rough work for more prosperous folk. She immediately put on a coarse apron, usually of sackcloth, and set about lighting a fire under the large copper in the wash-shed in the backyard, to supply copious supplies of hot water. While the water was heating, she and Mother sat down and drank cups of hot tea to brace them for the coming battle; they then began to sort out the clothes which had been steeping in a large tin bath overnight. Those requiring special treatment, being badly soiled, were scrubbed on the scullery table and rubbed on a zinc scrubbing-board. They were then ready for the poss tub. A poss tub is a large, stout, wooden barrel with an open top, usually about three feet in height. It was half-filled with boiling water from the copper, using a zinc bailer; some powdered soap was added and the clothes thrown in.

Now came the really heavy work of possing. This was done with a crude instrument called the poss stick, which consisted of a stout wooden pole two and a half inches in diameter and three feet long, with a crosspiece at the top for handling, and at the business end a heavy lump of wood shaped something like a huge thimble five inches thick and a foot long. There was a hole six inches deep bored in the bottom, and three slits in the side. In use, the washerwoman grasped the handle and proceeded to bash the clothes in the tub with an up and down movement. After about fifteen minutes of this rude treatment, the dirt in them emerged and floated on the top of the water, mixed with soap suds, which were skimmed off with a ladle; then the clothes were fished out with wooden tongs. It was heavy work, especially if several tubs of clothes had to be done, and there was more to come, as each item had to be wrung out by hand – two persons were required if sheets and blankets were in the wash. They were then put through the mangle, referred to in other parts of England as a wringer. This was a massive piece of machinery in those days, sometimes four feet high, made of a cast-iron frame supporting two heavy wooden rollers three feet in length and six inches thick, which could be adjusted to vary the pressure on the clothes fed between them. They had engaging iron cog-wheels at each end and were turned by a large iron wheel with a wooden handle set at right angles to the rim. As the items were fed through the rollers, cascades of water fell from them into a tub, and I loved to watch this process, but was never allowed to participate because mangling was a dangerous operation, and the operator had to take care not to get fingers caught between the rollers. Sometimes the clothes had to be put through several times at different pressures to squeeze out as much water as possible. After this, they were hung out to dry in the backyard; but as it frequently rained on washing days, they were hung on immense wooden clothes-horses in front of the kitchen fire shutting off the heat from members of the household. On particularly cold days, a fire was lit in the living-room, but even then a smaller clothes-horse for small articles was placed in front of it. Those who were

A paternal and a maternal uncle. 7 (*left*): The author's Uncle Archie (Peacock), a lieutenant in some 'very irregular cavalry'. The photograph is believed to be pre-Boer War. 8 (*right*): Uncle John (Briggs) in about 1880. He and his father owned the tug *Briton* in partnership with another relative, Uncle John Haire (not actually a direct uncle of the author's). They used it to haul wherries on the Tyne.

not fortunate enough to have a backyard hung out their washing in the back lanes and had to rush out several times a day to raise up the clothes line to allow the passage of coal carts, whose drivers were considerate enough to give warning by shouting "Coal coming".

Oddly enough, some women seemed to take a delight in combat with the washing, similar to warriors ardent for battle; but for the males in the household washing day was one of dread, because the females were usually short-tempered till the day was fought and won. The chorus of a well known folk song describes the atmosphere succinctly:-

"It is splash slash souse souse scrub scrub away
There's nowt but glumpin* in the hoose
On a rainy washing day."

Naturally, with all this activity going on, meals were secondary considerations, so dinner on Mondays usually consisted of the remains of the Sunday joint hastily warmed-up with "bubble and squeak" as vegetables. The whole house was filled with steam, the smell of soap, and the odour of drying clothes, which I can recall to this day with nausea.

Though the main battle against soiled clothes was fought on Mondays, the campaign went on during the week, and consisted of other engagements such as starching, ironing (iron flat-irons were used, and these were heated by propping them up on the fire bars), airing and folding; and finished on Fridays so that we could all have spotless linen to wear for the weekend. Nearly all white clothes were starched, particularly dickeys and detachable collars and cuffs, which were permissible wear for men in those days. Mother had firm ideas for the correct wear for her family, especially the males, and derided celluloid collars and cuffs except for the very young boys. I wore a celluloid Eton-type collar when at school but was promoted to a starched linen one on grand occasions.

My memories of my boyhood days reach back to the meals provided on the different days of the week which varied only a little according to the seasons of the year. Though not epicurean food, it was usually palatable and sustaining, and probably better than in many households of our class, perhaps because Father was

*short temper and growling

24

a provision merchant, and as Mother always had to pay him, she got the best quality. As a constant regular customer of a butcher who supplied the family for many years, we received odd bits of meat, called offal in those days, gratis. These consisted of such items as sheep's heads, liver, sheep's heart, ox tongue (at Christmas), chitterlings and fresh blood to make black pudding, tripe, kidneys, and sweetbreads – if we would accept them – as the latter were disdained by most persons except foreigners. Most butchers then owned their own shops, did their own slaughtering, were usually reasonably prosperous, and could afford to be generous. Even the very poor could afford some type of meat, even if only offal, and it is strange that meat is now becoming a luxury, and many folk have qualms in tasting black pudding because they have discovered that it is made of blood. It used to be made in our house and many others, and possibly still is in the North Country, in a pie dish with some simple ingredients added, then baked in an oven. I was always an addict and still am, if it is obtainable. Even now, when visiting Newcastle, I buy it in thick sausage form from a well known butcher in the market renowned for this "delicacy". Another tasty dish, which is now rarely made because butchers will not supply the ingredients, was potted meat. This was made in a porcelain basin of cow heel and odd bits of meat and eventually turned out as a kind of fleshy jelly, which was most nourishing and akin to the expensive calves' foot jelly sold in high class shops nowadays. Ham shank and pease pudding was another cheap meal as the meaty part was obtained free or for a few pence. There was nearly always enough meat on the bone to provide a portion for everyone in the family, and as the pease pudding had been boiled in a cloth with it, that tasted of ham. Mothers who had to provide a meal very economically used to make an enormous suet pudding (the suet was possibly free from the butcher) made with flour, salt, herbs, and water, boiled in a cloth, and announce that those who ate most pudding and onion sauce, which was poured over it, would be given most meat. No one who consumed several cubic inches of this pudding had much appetite for the next course.

Most puddings, served either as a main course or as a second one, were made solid to fill up empty stomachs. Mother's rice, sago or tapioca pudding were almost of the texture of lead because she added an egg to them, so that they were cut in slices and were only palatable if one ate them with added jam and milk. No one knew anything about cooking rice in the Eastern fashion and serving it as an addition to meat. One abominable pudding was occasionally served, and I still shudder at the thought of it. This was seed tapioca which the children called bullets, because it had the appearance and consistency of gelatinised grape-shot, and was reluctantly forced down the throat as plates had to be cleared to prevent waste. The only child who could avoid eating it was Nellie, who always had a queasy stomach and could be sick at will.

On the subject of wasted food, there was an expression used by Mother and my elder sister, but always by initial letter – B.B.B. than G.F.S. – as it was coarse. It meant "better belly burst than good food spoil" – so we had to eat up all that was set before us.

The main meal of the day in nearly all North Country households was midday dinner unless it was impossible for the bread-winner to come home at that time. If he could not come home because he was working in the pits or a factory, he took with him from home his "bait" which consisted of substantial sandwiches of cheese or cold meat, perhaps a small pie; and a can of tea which he warmed up, if possible, at work. Thermos flasks had not yet been invented, and created quite a stir – as a sort of miracle – when they were first put on the market. High tea was the next important meal for males, and consisted of some sort of meat or fish, the latter often tinned salmon which was then not as expensive as it is now, plus bread and butter, and granny loaf which consisted of bread made with brown flour sprinkled with raisins, currants and lemon peel. It was a substantial meal, but so that no one died of starvation during the night a supper of cheese, sweet biscuits and some left-overs, washed down with cocoa, was provided for the elders of the family.

The females frequently had afternoon tea, often called "a sly cup" if callers came. There is little doubt that females in those days were tea addicts, because a kettle was always on the hob so they could make a cup of tea quickly at any excuse, and certainly any lady calling at any time of the day would have been insulted if not offered a cup and a piece of cake. Coffee was rarely used as a beverage. Our bread, of course, and most scones or cakes, were always home baked, and anyone in these days who has not smelled the odour of baking bread, and experienced the taste of it fresh from the oven, has missed two of the good things of life. The bread was so good that growing boys could easily dispatch a fresh loaf at a sitting; so when flour became scarce during the wars, the Government forbade the sale of bread before it was a day old.

With the assistance of my older brothers, I have set down the following list of fare covering a week of dinners:

Sunday – a substantial joint of beef or mutton with Yorkshire pudding, followed by fruit tart. The basis of the latter was always apple, this being the cheapest fruit, with the addition of blackcurrants, cranberries, blackberries, etc.

Monday – this was a sparse day, as the women folk had little time to cook anything substantial, so we ate the leavings of Sunday dinner with the vegetables as bubble and squeak. To make up, we usually had kippers for high tea, great fat juicy ones from Scotland or Craster on the Northumberland coast, recognised world-wide for their flavour.

Tuesday – Sheep's head (referred to as sheep's Jimmy) broth with lots of barley in it, followed by the meat on the skull including the tongue; ginger pudding with treacle for afters.

Wednesday – suet pudding with onion sauce and Lancashire hotpot.

Thursday – steak and kidney pudding boiled in a basin wrapped in a cloth, followed by solid rice pudding and jam.

Friday – boiled cod and parsley – horrible for children, followed by treacle tart.

Saturday – ham shank with pease pudding done in a bag of mutton cloth (sheep carcasses at the butchers were wrapped in a fine gauze covering), followed by tapioca pudding.

Sundays in our home were so different from weekdays, that even at the early age of three I knew instinctively as soon as I awoke that it was the Sabbath, and I should remain in bed till the rest of the family was stirring. The terrace and houses were hushed and still, and when parents and older children arose later than

9: The author at about the age of five years.

10: The author's two brothers setting off on an expedition to the Lake District with a friend, in the decade before the First World War.

was usual during the week, the curtains would be only half-drawn. There were no tradesmen or passers-by on the pavements until it was time to go to church. Breakfast was later and taken more leisurely, and Father would skilfully cut the top of his boiled egg and present it to me for consumption. It was some years before I was promoted to a full ration of an egg for breakfast; and until I was older still, the meat in it would be turned out into a saucer for easier eating. Children were forbidden to crack the tops of boiled eggs and pick off little pieces, as this was counted as rather vulgar – tops must be cleanly sliced off.

Father never opened his shop on Sundays, and would have been excommunicated from our Presbyterian Church if he had, so he had time to read a newspaper at Sunday breakfast, not a proper newspaper but the *Christian Herald*, this being the only suitable one for the Sabbath as it was printed on Saturday. Mother read *The War Cry*, the Salvation Army weekly, as she was always inclined toward robust evangelical religion. Neither of them had any qualms in reading the Monday morning newspapers which were printed on Sunday evening. When I was older, and a cheeky schoolboy, I pointed this out to Father, and got a scolding instead of a proper explanation.

Reading-matter for children was strictly limited to the Bible, and one or two pieces of literature supposedly elevating and educational. They included Bunyan's *Pilgrim's Progress*, and we possessed a very large edition, about the size of a family album, with large print, and fearsome illustrations which frightened me when a child. Perhaps this limitation to good classical reading gave me a taste for it at an early age, though I would read *Comic Cuts* if I got the chance when away from home. When I look up at my infantry sword hanging above my writing desk, I am reminded of two literary quotations I memorised early in life from *Pilgrim's Progress*: "my sword shall go to him that can get it", and, "all the trumpets sounded for him on the other side".

Romping games were also barred and there was to be no singing of popular songs, though hymns were permitted.

Let it not be thought that our parents were more strict and puritanical than the majority; most church-going persons behaved similarly, and even young children became steeped in custom, remembering the Sabbath day to keep it holy, so that our games on Sunday evenings, when no parents were present, were imitations of our elders' conduct. Frequently, we played at "schools" or "church" led by my eldest brother, Alec, as teacher or preacher who examined us on various topics after reading a piece of the Bible or some good book. Looking back it is surprising that we did not all turn into little prigs, and perhaps not surprising that in adult life some of us, though believing in the tenets of Christianity, are laggard in church-going.

It may seem incredible in the present free-thinking and permissive society that the observance of the Sabbath, and attendance at divine worship and Sunday School, was then such an important factor in our lives. Indeed, as I have quoted in my autobiography *Tinker's Mufti*, when I returned on leave from the Western Front in World War One, one of the first questions put to me by my mother was "What did the soldiers do on Sundays?" It was some time before I could convince her that fighting proceeded as usual, and the previous Sunday night I had spent crawling about "no man's land" in front of our trenches.

One amusing and quiet game we did play on Sundays, when Mother was absent, was fishing with small rods and bent pins as hooks. The fishing ground was the bottom of her store cupboard which had a sunken floor. The fish were boots, which in those days always had tags at the heel to assist in drawing them on. The object was to hook these tags with the bent pin and haul them out of the cupboard, which was dark inside, making the fishing more difficult. (Shoes were a rarity in those days as male and female footwear was boots – I never wore shoes until I became an officer in the army, except for what were called sand-shoes (plimsolls) for use on the sea-shore.

Sundays sometimes ended with a flourish when visitors from the church congregation visited our home to sing lusty hymns round our piano, and oddly enough I feel sure these induced in me a liking for soldiers and a military career, because they were nearly all about preparing for battle – "fighting the good fight", "putting one's armour on", "lifting high the royal banner", "putting evil to flight with sharp swords" or "marching off to war" and "holding the fort". With few exceptions, the tunes were cheerful and the lyrics stirring, many from Moody and Sankey's hymnal. Everybody knew them, they being the pop tunes of the time, so it was not surprising that during the First World War the soldiers put their own words to them and they were sung far more frequently than *It's a long way to Tipperary.*

My mother loved the rousing tunes as she had been brought up to a sort of evangelical atmosphere and proclaimed, as did the Salvation Army "why should the devil have all the best tunes?"

We were not addicted to much praying, and there were no family prayers, as in some households; but certainly all members were expected to kneel at our bedside and say anything appropriate. Sister Edith, perhaps the most Christian of us all, saw to it that the younger children never omitted to do so.

We were taught to seek help from above in times of stress and trouble, sometimes in a curious way by allowing a Bible to fall open by itself and reading some of the script which might be applicable. Mother used a little box, now in my possession, containing hundreds of texts rolled up in little cylinders. After closing one's eyes and asking silently for guidance, one of these was picked out and then read. It was rather like consulting an oracle, because the meaning of the text was sometimes obscure and frequently seemed to have little bearing on the advice sought; but was always a comfort.

CHAPTER FOUR

Front Streets and Back Lanes

As I sit at my writing desk I can glance out of my study window into a quiet cul-de-sac in outer London, and feel that though it is pleasant enough, it is a dull scene compared with the front street and back lane of Cheltenham Terrace as I remember them. With the exception of Sundays, there was always something to interest a child, and always somebody about, passers-by or foot or on bicycles; Mrs. Potts holystoning her doorstep or Mrs. Ridley swilling and cleaning the pavement in front of her house with a long, hard brush, as she was houseproud; and there were always tradesmen. In my opinion, the streets were more colourful when I was a boy because many persons were in the uniform of their trade. The postman came three times a day and wore a smart, blue tunic and trousers with a red stripe down the legs, and what I thought an enviable head-dress, a kepi similar to that of an old-fashioned French soldier, with a peak back and front which turned the rain from his face and neck. I once thought of becoming a postman just so that I could wear such a cap. The Cheltenham Terrace postman carried a large sack over his shoulders in which were parcels as well as letters; and one of my first girl friends, aged six, informed me confidentially that he also had babies in it which he delivered to those who wanted them. I also envied telegraph boys who wore a smart uniform with a pill-box hat.

Butchers' boys were dressed in blue and white vertical-striped aprons and carried the meat in shallow, oblong, wooden platters with short handles at each corner on one shoulder. The meat was rarely covered except by a piece of mutton cloth, so one could detect whether neighbours were going to have a leg of mutton or a round of beef for dinner. Grocers' boys wore bibbed aprons in white and carried immense wicker-baskets on the crook of one arm. They usually wore flat cloth-caps which they dipped in flour before leaving the shop for no particular reason I can guess except to indicate their occupation.

Once a week a muffin man appeared, in a baker's apron and carrying a wooden tray similar to the butcher boy, and continually shook a large handbell to indicate his presence. He usually had little difficulty in selling his muffins because in those days a muffin was large and flavoursome, so different from those pieces of dough masquerading as muffins nowadays.

The milkman came, in white coat and apron, and with a milk float so constructed that the floor was only about a foot from the ground and open at the back, and I fancied it was like a Roman chariot. It contained two large milk churns on gimbals so that they could be canted to fill smaller hand churns from brass taps. It was drawn by a docile horse, whose reins passed over a metal bar at the apron of the vehicle. There were little bells or metal discs on this bar which jingled when the float was moving, giving notice of its presence in the street. Leaving the float, the milkman carried a small churn from door to door and filled customers' jugs with two little bailers carried in the churn. There was no bottled milk, and pasteurisation was only coming into fashion, so the milk was straight from the cows. It was better than pasteurised but found to be a possible cause of tuberculosis.

The milkman's horse was as welcome and well-known as the milkman himself, and followed him down the street pausing at the doors of customers which it knew as well as its driver. It was also perfectly aware that it would be patted and given titbits by children who had begged bread or apples from their mothers.

Nurses and midwives were constant passers-by, and they all wore colourful outfits with starched cuffs and collars and Dolly Varden bonnets with ribbons flying. There was an army depot in Newcastle, and frequently warships in the Tyne – the famous H.M.S. Calliope was moored as a training shop for the R.N.V.R. – so soldiers and sailors were often seen in the street. The military were always in blue or scarlet uniforms with pill-box hats canted over the right ear and carried silver-topped swagger canes; the sailors were in blue blouses and bell-bottomed trousers with the traditional sailor cap, but, if it was summer time, they might appear in white uniforms with large straw hats with flying ribbons.

Foot policemen were frequently to be seen in high-collared tunics and tall helmets, with heavy leather belts about their waists, to each of which was attached a large oil "dark" lantern and truncheon. At night the lantern was lit, but the light was concealed by

11: The Peacock family in about August 1911. Back row, left to right: Eleanor, Alex, Edith, Jim; centre: James Peacock, Jennie, Mrs Jenny Peacock; front: Basil.

a revolving shutter which could be turned if illumination was necessary – hence the name "dark" lantern. Oddly enough, a similar type was carried by burglars before the advent of electric torches. Police constables on their beats were much more numerous than they are today, and much more in evidence, as they often lived in the area which they patrolled, and were known and generally respected, by the residents, who valued the watch and ward they kept, knowing that a few blasts on a whistle in emergency would ensure prompt assistance from other members of the force. Except in areas where there were known criminals and wrong doers, vandalism was rare, as mischievious youths knew the policemen were likely to detect them in misdoing and administer immediate punishment by clouts over the head or whacks with the belt, followed by being led by the ear to their parents for further action. Persistent misdoing by boys could frequently lead to appearance before a magistrate and their being sent to a Training Ship where discipline was hard, continuous, and reforming.

Other characters who appeared in our front street wearing traditional costume of their trade were Cullercoats fish wives, coming to sell really fresh-caught sea food. Their costume, which had a kind of seafaring appearance, consisted of a heavy blue serge skirt, blouse and cowl of the same material, and the suggestion of a sailor's collar at the back, terminating with thick woollen stockings and stout boots. They carried their wares in a large wickerwork creel on their backs, with a supporting strap round the forehead and basket, and on one arm.

They came to the front doors, greeting prospective customers with "Ye'll be wantin' some bonny fine caller fish or a crab hinny catched this early morn?" If a sale was made, they produced a thick wooden board, placed a large fish on it and gave it a tap on its head to indicate it might be still alive, and then filleted it whilst sitting on the doorstep if they had not been invited inside the house to take a cup of tea, which they always poured into a saucer; or preferably a glass of beer if offered. They were amusing conversationalists and rather fun to have in the kitchen if they left their creels outside. They had a hard life selling their wares, which had been caught by the inshore fishermen (their husbands and sons) trudging many miles carrying heavy loads. The prices they charged, which were open to bargaining, were cheaper than those in a fish shop – ridiculously cheap – herrings were sometimes six for a penny, and a large crab fourpence. These Cullercoats folks were a distinctive clan, and rarely married outside it. They had the slatey blue eyes, the colour of the sea in front of their cottages. They were not usually tall in stature but very tough in physique. I know of two wives (one of whom supplied our household for years) who, while trudging the streets of Newcastle for miles in late pregnancy, gave birth to their babes, one during and the other immediately at the completion of their rounds. Many fisherfolk families were deeply religious folk, ardent supporters of chapel or church, and the men were lay preachers, who did much good in their time. Some fish wives were buxom, ruddy-cheeked ladies who could take their liquor and swear as well as any first mate in a sailing ship. Some of them, after disposing of their fish, would visit several pubs on their way home, and according to a friend of mine who used to travel with one when a small boy, frequently had to be assisted to the end of their journey. Most were mistresses of invective, if annoyed, and usually got the better in arguments. There is a well-known anecdote about a buxom one travelling in a crowded train to the coast. She had to stand, bearing her creel on her back, and noted that a man had risen to give his seat to a bonny young lass. Addressing the rest of the passengers in a loud voice, she exclaimed "Ye bugger, if I was like hor, and not all arse and tits, some young chap would lowp up and give *me* his place."

Different kinds of tradesmen appeared in the back lane and called at back doors. Coalmen covered with the dust of their trade were often dressed in the working garb of pitmen, short greyish collarless fustian jackets and "hodders" (short trousers fastened below the knee with a lace) and thick woollen stockings and boots.

Coopers in fustian trousers tied at the knees came periodically, and had a peculiar tuneful street cry –

"Any jobs for the cooper
Any tubs to mend."

Coopering was a necessary trade, especially for the repair of poss tubs, and any other wooden containers, because metal ones were almost unknown.

Fish vendors, not so romantic as fish-wives, came pushing flat barrows, usually in times of a glut of herrings, and it was possible to obtain twelve or more for a penny, as they had often obtained their supplies from boats at the quayside of North Shields at sixpence per bucketful sold to them by members of their crews. Herrings, now that the North Sea has almost been fished out, are something of a luxury away from the coast, which is a great pity as they were nourishing, cheap food for poor people who could ill afford much meat.

Pathetic rag-and-bone men came with little barrows or donkey carts, crying in musical, descending cadence: "Rags, bottles or bones for pennies." Alas, pennies were rarely passed over, but children might receive a toy ballon. All the items had some value to the collectors – the rags to be turned into shoddy cloth, the bones to make glue, and the bottles to be used again.

Knife grinders with highly coloured one-wheeled barrows were frequent callers, as knives and other cutting instruments required sharpening at short intervals, because few of them in an ordinary household were made of stainless steel. The process of grinding was generally viewed by a crowd of children, fascinated to see the sparks fly, and watch the operator treadle his lathe.

During the summer months, the terrace was visited by German bands, groups of itinerant musicians from "The Fatherland" dressed in field-grey or blue uniforms and wearing small peaked caps similar to those worn by German Army N.C.O.s. They played well, mostly marching-tunes or waltzes, and intrigued the children, as they were foreigners and came from across the sea and talked in a strange, different language.

Looking back, I wonder how they made enough money to pay their fares to and from England and support themselves, as the collections they made consisted mainly of coppers. Later, when the First World War began, many people affirmed that they had been spying-out the land as well as playing tunes all over England. A popular song during my boyhood, supposedly sung by a love-lorn English maiden who had been deserted by one of a band was:

Has anyone seen a German band, German band, German band?
I've been looking around all upon my own
I've searched every street both near and far, near and far,
Ya ya yah –
I want my Fritz who plays twiddly bits on his great trombone.

It should be realised by younger readers that in those days ordinary

12: Blackfriars, Newcastle (in about 1890), where the author's father attended a 'mission school' in the middle of the nineteenth century (see p. 11).

folk had little opportunities to hear music except in church or at a music hall, because few people had musical instruments, gramophones were still rare, and, of course, there was no taped music. So, cheerful noise in the streets was welcome, and itinerant persons who came with barrel organs or mechanical pianos were appreciated. Organ grinders came, with a small instrument supported on one wooden leg and with a mangy monkey sitting on top; which was a great diversion, though the poor beast usually looked miserable and sometimes vicious.

Dark-haired men came in pairs, and one played a hurdy-gurdy – an instrument resembling a large musical-box played by turning a handle, while his partner persuaded a medium-sized brown bear attached to a chain to get up on its hind legs and dance to the music. It was a sorry sight, as the animal could only be persuaded by poking it with a stick, and tender-hearted children rushed away to beg a bun from their mothers to reward it.

Certainly, the most exciting incident in our terrace was a carthorse falling down in the road. This often happened in winter because of ice on the granite sets, and always collected a crowd of adults and youngsters. The poor beast, very frightened, usually struggled to get up, raising its head and kicking out vigorously with its hind hooves, entangling itself further in its traces and cart shafts. The carter, perturbed but not dismayed, would call for his boy, or an interested bystander, to sit on the horse's head, pressing it to the ground, and this odd procedure nearly always resulted in the animal lying still. Willing hands then loosened all its harness and detached the traces, then pulled the cart back to free the shafts. Sacks were placed round or underneath the horse, if possible, to give its hooves a better grip on the granite sets; then the carter, holding the bridle close to the bit, told the person sitting on the animal's head to get up quickly. As soon as he did so, the horse struggled up on to its four legs, and stood trembling with fright until calmed by patting, stroking and soft words.

Funeral cortèges in those days usually started from the deceased's home, as there were few funeral parlours provided in the undertaker's establishments; so an occasional one took place in the terrace.

People were taken to cemeteries and interred with much more ceremony than at present, and every houshold nearby paid respect by pulling down the blinds facing the front street, and usually peeped through a chink to observe the coffin being brought out and placed in the hearse. This was a grand black equipage, glass-sided, with elaborate carving on the woodwork and on the roof, and plumes at each corner. It was drawn by a pair of magnificent, finely groomed horses with plumes of black and silver feathers rising between their ears. Their harness, all black leather, was highly polished and the metal pieces burnished. The deceased made his last journey in great pomp.

The local band of the Salvation Army marched into our terrace early on Sunday mornings, before it was time to go to church. The uniforms were very similar to those of soldiers of the time, but the tunics were a duller red than scarlet. With their instruments burnished bright, they played cheerful tunes, some of them taken from the music hall ditties with different words. The lasses carried tamborines and certainly seemed to enjoy shaking and striking them.

After one or two hymns, the leader exhorted everyone to fight evil and the Devil, and also onlookers to throw pennies on the big drum which had been placed face upwards on the ground. As onlookers did so, the leader would count the number and announce it, and pray for more, rather like an auctioneer asking for further bids; but when the pennies stopped, the band would form up and move on to the next street.

If a wedding reception took place in one of the houses, crowds of boys would gather waiting for the bride and bridegroom to emerge and drive away in a carriage to begin their honeymoon. If the weather was fine, the carriage would have the hood down, so every bystander could glimpse the newly-weds, and the boys would run alongside it singing:

"Hi canny man hoy* a hapenny oot
A wedding's great fun there is no doot [doubt]
Wherever ye gan ye'll hear us shoot.
He canny man hoy a hapenny oot."

It was a very parsimonious groom who did not respond and throw out a handful of coppers as largess.

Cheltenham Terrace had interest for me all day, terminating in the arrival of the lamplighter, with his staff which had a flame

*Hoy – Geordie dialect for throw.

40

burning in a metal tube at the top. He came at about the time I was going to bed, and, as a sensitive child, I used to repeat the words of a Sunday School hymn: "Now the day is over, night is drawing nigh, shadows of the evening steal across the sky", as I watched the gas lamps ignite with a plop, and shine yellow in the growing darkness.

CHAPTER FIVE

Respectability and Gentility

It was the earnest wish of most people in those distant days to be looked upon as respectable, and if possible genteel, unless, because of acute poverty, they had to give up the struggle to attain these objectives. The conduct and many activities of persons of the lower middle class were restricted and circumscribed by the phrase "What will the neighbours think?" The upper and the depressed classes rarely cared what the neighbours thought, and lived untrammelled by the conventions which hedged about life in my family and others.

From early days, parents taught and admonished their offspring that they could only rise in the world by industry, good conduct and self-help, and if they did not aspire to higher status, they would perhaps end up in the workhouse. The well-known book Smiles' *Self Help* which gave a good counsel and maxims which would lead to success in life was almost as widely read as the Bible, and books of etiquette which included the supervision of butlers, housemaids, etc., were popular reading for females. Servants were plentiful in those days, and even modest households such as ours sometimes employed domestic help, usually young girls who were known as "skivvies".

Nearly every child, poor or rich, knew the difference between good and evil, because they received some religious instruction, sometimes willynilly, since all charitable institutions believed that the tenets of Christianity should be served with free meals or other bounties. The large majority of children of all classes attended Sunday Schools, even if they came from what is termed now "problem families" as their irreligious parents wanted them out from under their feet on the Sabbath, a day of resting after a hard week's work and Saturday drinking. Though they were lax in obeying the ten Commandments, most children, and many adults, believed they were in danger of hell fire in the future if they were wicked.

It is a truism that intelligent children coming from a poor or deprived home have much greater difficulty improving their station in life than those coming from good homes with ambitious parents do. We were lucky, in our family, as we had both. Not only were our parents ambitious for their children's future, but denied themselves many comforts, and some necessities, to that end. Mother was indefatigable in pushing us upwards, and Father spent less on himself than any man I know, so that we could benefit from good education. He never smoked, drank or spent money on entertainment till late in life. He never amassed many wordly goods, but was highly respected.

The first step to attaining respectability was to ensure that all the children were tidily clothed, and perhaps a little better than their neighbours. Our clothing was never soiled nor tattered, like many of our school mates, but carefully darned or patched if necessary. Our faces were washed and made shining, and if I had been remiss in washing, a dirty neck was liable to be scrubbed with pumice powder. The next step was that of speech. At home we were discouraged from speaking that Geordie dialect which is almost incomprehensible to southerners, but I had to speak it communicating with my playmates, otherwise I would have been dubbed a snob, and a bit cissy. All the family, however, retained the Northumbrian brogue and tone in their speeach, which is almost impossible to eradicate. Any Northumbrian being a successful in doing so is still looked upon as "putting it on", swanking and ashamed of his birthplace.

One of the easiest ways of attaining respectability and higher status for people of modest means, was to train as a teacher, because the training was inexpensive and there were scholarships for the gifted pupils. Training and study for other professions, such as medicine, dentistry, the law, or commissions in the armed forces, was much more expensive, and beyond the means of lower-middle-class parents. A schoolmaster or school-mistress in those days was looked upon as a person of considerable education, and expected to conduct himself or herself in a sedate and sober manner, and also to dress becomingly without flamboyance.

Two brothers and one sister of mine became teachers, and if it had not been for the advent of the First World War, I, too, might have ended up in the profession. A short period as a pupil teacher directed to instruct pupils who were more advanced in learning

43

13: Grainger Market, Newcastle's covered market, in about 1920 (see p. 11).

than myself decided me never to continue my studies and qualify. Mother was responsible for aiming to have a fourth member of the family as a teacher, but fortunately for myself and my pupils, I escaped by absconding and joining the army under age. Sister Eleanor became a librarian when that profession was opened up to females and counted a very lady-like profession. My eldest and beloved sister, Edith, was the "Martha" in the family, much too useful to be allowed to train for a profession, and the rest of us owe her a great debt.

I still marvel that Father and Mother were able to support their children during training for their professions. Though we gained scholarships which covered college fees, we had to be kept, fed and decently clothed, without bringing in any money for the family purse. Many less dedicated parents would have given up the struggle and sent us out to work. Naturally, as was the practice in those days, clothes were handed down from older children to younger ones, as with our modest income from Father's business, it was impossible to buy new outfits for all of us. Being the youngest, I was the last to suffer from cut-down clothes.

Before 1914, there were few of the items of dress now termed leisure clothes or play suits, except coloured blazers for rich folk, but most men and boys had a stiff straw hat, or boater, for wear in summer, which for no reason I can discover was called "a benger", now rarely seen worn except by Harrovians or duo tap dancers on the music-hall stage.

I never saw my father, either in our house or out of it, except in respectable suit, starched shirt collar and cuffs. For business, he wore detachable cuffs and a dickey, then quite a respectable item in any man's wardrobe. In our home, it was forbidden to sit about in shirt sleeves, or with braces showing, as this was counted as a working class custom. A wife of a working man or artisan would announce to her husband on his return from work: "Get your coat off, lad, your dinner's ready".

Saucering one's tea was also forbidden, though it was a constant practice of many elderly folk. It was reported by sister Eleanor, with some disdain, that a friend of hers, having asked her boy friend to tea one day, beseeched her grandmother to refrain from doing so as he would think badly of her relative, but the old lady was obstinate and declared "Lad or nee lad aa'l saucer me tea as usual".

We were forbidden to refer to what is now called "the loo", as the "netty", this being a lower class term, and even "W.C." was frowned upon. Closet was acceptable; or, even more delicately, "washing one's hands in the little room upstairs" was talked of.

Whistling or singing except on occasions accompanied by the piano was *de trop*, and I can remember Mother getting mad at me when I was quite a young lad, for repeatedly murmuring the ditty which was popular at the time "Casey Jones, mounted on his engine, and took his farewell trip into the promised land". Mother objected not only to the singing, but the irreligious mention of the Promised Land in a music hall song.

All respectable people in our stratum of society attended some place of worship, and their social, as well as religious, life centred about church or chapel. They had many denominations to choose from. In addition to Roman Catholicism and the established Church of England, there were innumerable nonconformist sects, all of which attracted large congregations. To name a few: there were missions of several sorts, mainly with lay preachers, Methodists, Primitive Methodists, Wesleyans, Congregationalists, Christian Scientists, Presbyterians (established or unestablished), and Unitarians, who decline to believe in the Trinity, but recognise one God with Jesus as his prophet. The established Church of England in Northern industrial towns was the church of upper class or richer folk, and, curiously, regarded by devout chapel folk as verging on Catholicism. I remember when I earnestly wished to join a troop of Boy Scouts in 1908, when Lord Baden-Powell founded this admirable organisation, my parents forbade me to do so, because the local troop was located in Church of England premises.

The Roman Catholic churches were attended by the very rich or very poor people, and foreigners, which, in the belief of many Protestants, made them suspect.

Our family were members of the Presbyterian Church of England, akin to that of Scotland, which, as its name implies, is governed by the Elders. Our place of worship was within a few yards of Cheltenham Terrace, and entitled Heaton Presbyterian, which still functions with a fair congregation.

Its form of worship was not so Calvinistic as in Scotland but pretty strict. Oddly enough, I never discovered till late in life that my father who attended its services most of his adult life never became a full member, but called himself an adherent, because he could not subscribe to some of its tenets. Late in life he swung over to a Unitarian church. This was typical of Father, a man of great integrity, who could not dissemble or conceal his true feelings or opinions even if these were unpopular.

Unless illness precluded, Father, Mother and the older children attended morning and evening services. Almost as soon as they were weaned, the younger children attended Sunday School during the afternoons of the Sabbath, leaving the elders resting till our return at tea time. There was a less formal evangelistic school for children on one evening per week during winter months, called "The Band of Hope"; what we were hoping for I never discovered except perhaps to reach heaven. As we had hardly had time in our short lives to be really wicked, it seemed a little unnecessary, especially as we were taught to abjure intoxicating liquor to which we had no access. The meetings consisted of two or three children's hymns, a short moral discourse by an adult leader; then songs and recitations by members of the audience, some liking to show-off, and others press-ganged into performing. The talent was not very high, and even I, at the age of six, was cajoled into giving reci-tations. My final appearance, when I was old enough to acquire stage fright, leaves me embarrassed to this day when I think of it. Up to then my party *pièce de résistance* consisted of some verses entitled Jack Frost. Reluctantly, I had been placed on the platform when I wanted to make water, and the leader announced me as a very young, but accomplished reciter. I began "Jack Frost looked forth one starry night", then stood dumb-stricken with stage fright, and though prompted by members of the audience could not utter another word nor make an exit: then burst into tears and, with damp trousers, had to be lifted down by my elder brother.

I can still recall some of our popular Band of Hope hymns – "Jesus loves me this I know, because the Bible tells me so", and "When the roll is called up yonder, I'll be there". Another, "Jesus wants me for a sunbeam", I heard sung in peculiar circumstances decades later, whilst I was a prisoner of war, a captive of the Japanese on the River Kwai in Thailand. Our battalion comic, a middle-aged soldier used to make us laugh by singing it in a raucous and untuneful voice when called out by a Japanese guard for some job.

The songs rendered by other artistes at the meetings were so sentimental that today they could only be sung in mockery. I cannot recall one which was humorous; and at a very early age in life we were expected to meditate on deprived and unfortunate children, such as barefooted crossing sweepers, infant chimney sweeps, those with drunken parents, the crippled or blind. There were many of these unfortunates about, so sympathy for them was not misplaced. I vividly remember one young artiste who persistently sang "Won't you buy my pretty flowers" – it was difficult to prevent her doing so – and used to reduce me to tears when I was aged seven and very sensitive. The song is now a classic example of doleful ditties of the period.

"Underneath the gaslight glitter,
Stands a little fragile girl,
Crying through the night wind bitter,
'Won't you buy my pretty flowers?'
There are many sad and weary
In this pleasant world of ours,"etc.

Another tear-jerking one usually sung by an adult was –

"Where is my wandering boy tonight?
The heart of a father yearns
My heart o'er flows for nobody knows
Oh where is my boy tonight?"

One ditty which delighted me because it had to do with soldiers was called "Two little boys", and to my astonishment was resurrected by Rolf Harris, the Australian entertainer, a few years ago, and it became a hit record on "Top of the Pops". The second part of the song briefly relates the incident when one of two friends was wounded in battle and the other did not desert him, but lifted him on to his own horse saying "There is room on my horse for two", and probably gaining a decoration for his action.

There was a curious song about a chidren's quarrel, the cause of which I have never discovered to this day. I think it originated in the United States of America.

"I don't want to play in your yard,
I don't like you any more;
You'll be sorry when you see me

48

14: Shields Road, Byker, in 1901. Here the Peacock family lived before moving to Cheltenham Terrace, where the author was born. Here, too, was James Peacock's shop near to 'the growing and more genteel suburb of Heaton. . .' (see p. 14).

15: Another view of Shields Road, in about 1905.

Swinging on our garden door.
You won't play around our rain barrel,
You won't climb our apple tree;
I don't want to play in your yard,
If you won't be good to me!"

As a light relief from this misery, the whole assembly was directed
to sing about Noah's Ark:

Old Noah he wanted to build an ark;
There's one more river to cross;
And he covered it over with hickory bark.
There's one more river to cross:
One more river, and that's the River of Jordan;
One more river, there's one more river to cross.

Then:

The animals went in one by one,
There's one more river to cross.
The elephant and the kangaroo,
There's one more river to cross.

The rhyming couplets caused great amusement, especially –

The animals went in four by four,
The big hippopotamus stuck in the door.

And:

The animals went in six by six,
The monkey was up to his usual tricks.

We were easily amused in those days.

At special meetings, we were given a magic lantern show by
adults who possessed a type of apparatus that was more than a
toy. It was lit by acetylene, which smelt horrible. The pictures
were in colour, mostly stills of buildings and scenes from abroad,
so they were mainly educational and compered by a geography
teacher. Towards the end of the performance, several comical slides
were shown and figures on them moved. This was done by using

double glass slides, one of which was the background and with the figures on the other, which was moved by the operator by means of a little cog wheel. One, which depicted an old gentleman lying in bed with his mouth open and a series of mice jumping into it, brought down the house.

About 1906, we progressed from the magic lantern to moving pictures, and marvelled at the miracle of characters actually walking about on the screen. I marvelled so much that I can still remember details of the plot such as it was. We were told that the film had been made in France, and the characters were all foreigners. When projected, the picture was almost opaque, and though it depicted the inside of a drawing-room, the action seemed to be taking place in a rainstorm as celluloid films were very scratched. A man and a woman, obviously husband and wife, were waiting anxiously – this was indicated by gestures – wringing of hands, etc. Eventually the man put his hand to his ear, obviously listening, then went to the door and opened it. Two workmen doffing their hats appeared and indicated by gestures that they had brought something. They went out and after several minutes of suspense came back carrying a piano which was received with joy and almost ecstasy by the wife. It was placed in position and she sat down on a piano stool and began to play. A caption informed us of the piece being played as, naturally, the film was silent. The husband went to a sideboard and fetched a bottle of wine, and glasses. These were filled, with some ceremony, and the workmen toasted the husband and the piano, tossing off the wine at one gulp. They then departed and the husband and wife embraced as the scene faded.

The next film, however, was, and still is counted as a classic epic, entitled: *The Great Train Robbery*. This caused consternation amongst the audience, as one of the shots showed an enormous American locomotive approaching head on, and giving the appearance of coming off the screen into the hall. Several children, including myself, screamed, ducked below our seats and burst into tears. The only other incident I remember from the film was that of the brave station-master's daughter tapping out a message in morse to warn the police after her father had been tied-up by the robbers.

These film shows, in unprotected halls, were soon stopped by law following fires and casualties amongst children when projectors burst into flames.

In addition to Bands of Hope, other elevating entertainment for children was provided by meetings of The Sons (and Daughters) of Temperance. They were not held in our church but in one nearby – a Methodist, I think. Admission was free but collection was taken, so parents provided children with pennies. The object of the leaders of the organisation was to teach the children about the evils of alcoholic drink, and so enthusiastic were they that at the age of about eight, or earlier, infants were expected to sign a pledge to abjure alcoholic beverages and to learn that "wine was a mocker, and strong drink was raging". The majority of people today may be astonished that total abstainers should go so far as to persuade infants to foreswear beer, wine and spirits before many of them understood what alcohol was, but in the early Edwardian times strong drink was cheap, and a curse, especially amongst the poor, and several societies advocating temperance were in existence. My mother belonged to the British Women's Temperance Association, and constantly wore a pretty little badge made of enamel, in the form of a knot of white ribbon which was its emblem. Nevertheless, she was fond of preparing home-made beverages such as dandelion stout and ginger beer, quite innocently thinking them non-alcoholic though the stone jars in which they were made frequently blew their corks, due to the brisk fermentation of the ingredients. Most of these 'non-intoxicating' drinks must have contained more alcohol in them than any liquors produced in a distillery. They were consumed with contented smacks by Mother and her friends, many of whom were members of the British Women's Temperance Association.

Meetings of the Sons of Temperance were well attended, as some of the educational talks were accompanied by simple, chemical experiments illustrating the evils of alcohol, and professional entertainers gave performances of conjuring, ventriloquism and shadow graphs. The songs and hymns we were taught were more cheerful and tuneful than those in The Bands of Hope. I recall a few snatches of them –

My drink is water bright, water bright, water bright,
My drink is water bright from the crystal spring.

And another –

> I knew a man his name was Paddy Green,
> And a drunkard vile was he.

He was reformed by the words of a child, and the song finished with a rousing chorus –

> Till he threw down the bottle and the glass,
> And he picked up the pledge book and pen,
> And signed and signed and signed
> To be a sober man, man, man, and signed to be a sober man.

One recitation I recall described an unlikely incident. A very thirsty, bibulous traveller asked a young boy where he could get a drink, and was led to the village pump. Though dying to reach a public house, he was so impressed by the boy's action that, instead of giving him a clip over the ear, he immediately became a teetotaller and signed the pledge.

The Bands of Hope provided primary religious instruction for young children, but those in their middle teens continued their studies in Bible Classes. My father taught in one for many years with his customary earnest gravity, and I inherited a fine clock with an appropriate inscription which he received from his pupils on his retirement in 1912. It still goes, and keeps good time on my dining room mantelpiece. I now realise that many of his pupils did not attend solely for piety, or avid wish to study the Scriptures, but because the meetings gave them opportunities of meeting members of the opposite sex and walking home with them. In those days, opportunities of dalliance or chatting up the girls unchaperoned were rare, so many marriages were the result of Bible Class sessions. The regular services in our Presbyterian Church were normally grave and dull, but occasionally external ministers livened them up by delivering evangelistic sermons which dwelt on the terrible future of the wicked if they did not reform in time to escape hell fire. When I was ten years old, I attended a morning service and still remember it with some apprehension. An old clergyman who came from Scotland, and was probably a Wee Free Minister was in the pulpit. He was heavily bearded and hirsute, with staring eyes, and his appearance was alarming even before he began his sermon, because he stared at the congregation for several minutes before and after reading the text till there was complete silence, and we were all slightly mesmerised. He then smote the pulpit reading desk and delivered his sermon in a loud, threatening voice as though we were almost beyond salvation. The congregation was spell-bound as our own minister was a kindly, gentle man, so different from this one. Finishing his lengthy sermon with an exhortation for us to ask for mercy and to remember his portents, he then picked up the massive Bible in front of him and brought it down with a crash on the reading desk, startling us all, then, throwing his gown around him with a flourish, he sat down. One younger member of the congregation sitting in the front row of the gallery was so agitated that he knocked his Bible, a large one, over the rail, and it fell with a crash into the body of the Church. He then fled in terror of retribution and damnation.

As mentioned at the beginning of this chapter, our social life circled around the Church, whose members were all friends and acquaintances, so many of our amusements happened in the Church Hall. There were meetings for lectures and debates once a month and called The Guild, and occasional parties called soirées when food, tea and strictly non-alcoholic drinks were supplied. Adult amateur entertainers did their party pieces, vocally or on piano or violin. The ladies rendered "Songs of Araby", then quite new; "Just a song at twilight"; "I dream't I dwelt in marble halls"; "Home, sweet home", and such like. The gentlemen sang "Down amongst the dead men"; "Simon the cellarer", in surprisingly deep voices; "My old shako"; and "Wheel my chair to the window as the troops go marching by". The American Civil War was fresh in the minds of the older folk, so the soldier songs of that period such as "John Brown's body"; "Marching through Georgia"; and "Just before the battle, Mother", were popular. My father, who had steeped himself in Civil War history, used to recite Barbara Fletchie with actions – always part of a recitation in those days – and arms and head were constantly in motion during the act. Our minister, a kind man, approved of dancing, if of a refined nature, as he declared that the scriptures mention "David danced before the Lord"; so we pranced the Roger de Coverley, and "Push the business on", but no frivolous dances such as waltzes and polkas.

Though I have written lightly about our amusements connected with the Church, I trust readers will not think I ridicule them or that they were unenjoyable. We enjoyed them enormously as there were few entertainments which could be had so cheaply. Without them, our lives would have been dull indeed.

CHAPTER SIX

Outdoor Occupations

Except for those provided at schools, there were few children's playgrounds, and only well-to-do people had gardens, so we played in the streets and back lanes. There was little traffic except the occasional tradesmen's carts, so this was comparatively safe. Visits to municipal parks were rare, and then only during holidays, when family expeditions were organised, led by older children. It was customary to take some refreshment, in the form of sandwiches and buttered buns plus a bottle of pop, though if the latter was too expensive we took bottles of "Spanish water", a sickly concoction simply made by dissolving aniseed balls and liquorice in cold tap water. If we had any pocket money and visited Jesmond Dene, we bought an egg from a poor old woman who used to stand at one gate crying out "Boiled egg and a biscuit hinny all for a penny hinny".

Real sports kit was rare and if a boy owned a cricket bat or a leather football he was counted something of a plutocrat and given special consideration when playing, because if annoyed at some decision of the other players he was apt to stalk off the field carrying away the bat or ball. Normally, if playing in the street, the football consisted of newspapers tied up with string in a round bundle. If we played cricket, a lamp post was the wicket, the bat roughly fashioned out of a plank of wood, and the ball of solid rubber.

Most boys' games included a chase with pursuers and pursued. "Haraleavin" (I am guessing at the spelling phonetically; the word "hara" is probably ancient French meaning "come to assistance", and is sometimes used in the Channel Islands), a chase and rescue game, was most popular and played as follows:-

A large semicircle was drawn with chalk against a wall and represented a prison. Eight or more players were divided equally into two teams, and two from one side were placed in the prison. The other team acted as guards and also as pursuers of members

57

of the first team, to catch them and place them in prison. The members of that team, not already in prison, not only tried to avoid capture but also to release their comrades. This was done by running through the chalk bay touching a prisoner, and both running off without being touched or caught by members of the opposing team. The game was best played in semi-darkness so that the contestants could lurk in tactical positions in shadows to catch or release others. The prisoners in the bay would shout "haraleavin", to direct their rescuers, and the rescuers, suddenly bounding from darkness, would shout even louder, to startle the guards and avoid capture themselves. The game went on till exhaustion or until all of one side were captured or escaped. Then the sides changed their roles.

Another chasing game played in the dark was "Jack show your light". The rules were simple: one of the players was designated as "It" or "Jack" and carried a small, dark lantern, burning oil or a candle. This player was allowed some minutes' grace to run into the darkness and hide himself, keeping his lantern shaded. As few boys possessed a watch, the timing was done by counting to one hundred and fifty, then the pursuers shouted "Jack show your light", and Jack, in honour bound, exposed the light momentarily and ran away to another position. The pursuers knew this, and though one would run in the direction of the light, the remainder would scatter stealthily in the dark so that when "Jack" was called upon to show his light again he might inadvertently be close to a pursuer who could pounce and touch him. A player who was successful in touching him became "Jack", took the lantern, and the game went on.

One diversion called "heads", usually played in a school playground, was extremely simple but gave opportunities of bawling and general mayhem. It was obligatory for the players to be five or more, and uneven in numbers. They stood in a circle about three feet apart, then moved round anti-clockwise, singing "King Henry's boys go round, go round; a lump of lead, a crust of bread and everyone a head". At the final word every player tried to grab the head of another, and as there was an uneven number a slow player would not find a free head, became "It", and was mocked as such. The routine was repeated, and had no ending till the school bell summoned us again to classrooms. For the benefit of those who are ignorant of Tyneside dialect, I have written the words in English, but the players pronounced them as "King Henery's booys gan roond, gan roond, gan roond; a lump of leed a crust o' breed, and iveryone a heed".

Recently, when looking at Bruegel's famous painting of children's games four hundred years ago, I noticed that some players are engaged in this game and wonder at the derivation of it which must be connected with some historical episode. Though we were not aware of it at the time, King Henry VIII and the other famous Harry, of Northumberland, Harry Hotspur of Alnwick Castle, were still vaguely remembered because the expressions "By the great Harry" or "By the living Harry", were commonly used to indicate fervency or choler.

Another rough game, intentionally rough, was called "Mount the Cuddy", for which two teams of four or more were necessary. It was decided which side would be "on" first by tossing a coin or drawing lots in some way if no one had a coin. To be "on" was to provide the cuddy (horse) for the other team to mount. The weakest member of this team leant with his back to a wall and the others bent down heads to buttocks in succession to form the horses back, holding on to each other to make it strong. In position, the team had formed a sort of one-ended vaulting horse. Players of the other team in turn vaulted on the bent backs, scrambling as far as possible towards the wall to allow space for the others to mount. Their main purpose was to break the back of the Cuddy so that they came down on it with all their weight. If the Cuddy's back was not broken, the other side had to provide a Cuddy. It was rarely possible for the "on" side to bear up without breaking, and the real purpose of the game was for all the players to end up in a heap on the playground. It was a very strenuous pastime, and looking back I wonder how we escaped many serious injuries. We sustained lots of bruises, and our clothes suffered badly and had to be patched by patient mothers. Patched clothes were not a disgrace, but torn or ragged ones were, especially if they exposed a piece of shirt in the region of the buttocks.

For less strenuous pastimes, we played varied games of marbles. Most marbles were then made of pot (fired clay) – the glass ones were too expensive, and much prized if obtained. In addition to a pocketful of small ones, every lad had a "plonker", which was a large one used to pitch at the others. A cheap plonker could be obtained by breaking up a lemonade bottle and obtaining the glass

16: Heaton Road in about 1900.

17: Another view of Heaton Road and its tramway lines, in about 1905.

stopper which was used as a seal, a common practice before screw caps were invented. In addition to the normal game in which small marbles are placed inside a chalked circle and knocked out with plonkers, we played one which took place in the street gutters – one player, using his thumb and forefinger, would shoot a marble along a gutter as far as possible. His opponent then did the same, trying to hit the first marble, which he claimed if he did so. Then he would shoot first and the game went on the length of the street. The drain gratings were hazards, as ill-judged shooting led to marbles being lost forever down them. There was another version which necessitated making holes the size of marbles in bare ground about three feet apart. The rules were very complicated, but the main object was for players to shoot their plonkers into each hole in turn, and knock their opponents' marbles which had not been holed as far away as possible; rather akin to croquet, using the holes instead of hoops.

In addition to marbles there were other items of equipment which every boy aspired to possess for his own amusement. They were a "tip cat", a "clagger", and a "banger", all of which could be improvised at small expense. "Tip cat" is an ancient game, and still played with manufactured equipment in northern counties under the name of "Knurr and Spell". Home-made equipment consisted of a piece of wood about four inches long and an inch square, sharpened to a point at each end. This was the "cat", and in use was placed across a similar piece of wood which was unpointed, on the ground, one sharpened end upwards. Using a stout stick, this end was hit smartly and the tip cat jumped into the air and the player attempted to hit it, again with the stick, and drive it away as far as possible. It could be a dangerous pastime because if hit correctly the tip cat would fly immense distances, though in no particular direction, with great force, hazarding onlookers and nearby windows. A "clagger" was a peaceful sort of contraption, giving pleasure only to its handler. It consisted of a disc of real leather about four inches in diameter with a small hole bored at the centre, through which a long piece of string was passed and knotted on the under-side. The leather was then well wetted and pressed hard downwards on to a flagstone in the pavement, where it stuck firmly by suction. When the handler pulled the string hard upwards, the suction was relieved with a lovely, lewd, squelching noise, greatly appreciated by boys and deprecated by adults, which could be repeated at will at no expense. A "banger" was another apparatus which annoyed adults, not only because of the noise it made but because it was dangerous. It was really a homemade firework, an explosive device which made a much louder detonation than could be expected from its simple components. These components were, a large door key with a hollow shank, a large nail which could be slid inside it, and a piece of string about three feet in length, one end of which was tied to the key shank and the other tied near the head of the nail. The explosive consisted of the heads of "Puck" matches, which were not the safety kind. These were packed into the open end of the key and pressed down, half-filling the shank. The nail was now inserted, leaving the head and one inch of it protruding. To produce a detonation, the handler, holding the string in the middle, swung the contraption, nail first, hard against a brick wall, preferably round a corner. The point of the nail was thus driven into the match heads, which exploded with a satisfying loud bang. Daring lads used potash of nitre which could be bought at any chemists, mixed with a few grains of gunpowder from a real firework. Using these materials the device could be lethal, as they often made it burst like an over-charged gun. There was a simpler form of banger, not half so exciting, which consisted of two halves of a small sphere of metal threaded on a string. A percussion cap from a toy pistol was inserted between the pieces of metal and the two dropped on to the pavement, making a small detonation.

If we could obtain the parts, we used to make what we called "bogies", out of four small perambulator wheels on axles with a plank between them for a body. The body could be steered by fastening the front axle to a cross-piece of wood with only one iron bolt attaching it to the body, and the driver operated it by pulling on strings tied to its ends. These vehicles were our pride and joy, especially when used downhill. I once erected a mast and sail, made from a mackintosh coat, on my bogie, but had to remove them at the order of a policeman who said such a vehicle was not only dangerous to other road users but should be licenced. Bogies have now become "coasters", expensive toys turned out by manufacturers, but I feel ours gave us as much pleasure, as they were all our own work.

Our games in the streets usually ended when elder brothers and sisters chased us home, or when one of the players got tired of them and said so. His companions then sang mockingly: "Billy Billy buck, the game's broke up, all through Johnny Piper" – or whatever the name of the culprit was.

Many of our games were seasonable, and only played at certain periods of the year, but curiously no one seemed to be able to designate these periods. There was the marble season, the spinning-top season, and the banger season or tip cat season; and by some unfathomable instinct boys began playing these games almost on the same day as the first of the season. At times the streets would be void of marbles, spinning-tops, or bangers; then, within a few hours, would be full of them.

Bowling hoops was a popular pastime for both sexes in fine weather, but it was recognised that only girls and infant boys used wooden ones. The lads used types made of thin iron bar bent into a circle, with an iron baton with a hook at one end by which the hoop could be kept running upright for long distances.

Duckstone was a very ancient and popular game because it needed no equipment except a few pebbles or stones picked up from a piece of open ground. It was played as follows: each player selected a stone about the size of a hen's egg, and a large stone or brick was placed upright on the ground and called "the duck". Lots were drawn to appoint someone as "It" to begin the game. He placed his pebble on the "duck", and the remainder of the players retired behind a line about fifteen feet away from it. They then threw their pebbles in turn with the object of knocking "Its" pebble from the "duck". If they failed, they had to stand where their pebbles fell on the ground. As soon as some player with better aim succeeded in knocking off the target pebble, they could pick up their own and run back behind the line. "It" immediately had to replace his pebble on the "duck" and try to touch a player before he reached the safety line. If he did this player became "It", and had to place his pebble on the "duck". The game could be fast and furious, and a little dangerous because of flying pebbles, but it was good exercise for active boys. Oddly enough, the last time I saw this game played was by soldiers on "rest", behind the line on the Western Front in 1917.

As soon as children had advanced from the toddler stage there was strict sexual apartheid in outdoor games. I cannot remember any girl being permitted to join in any boys' games, except occasionally when visiting the seaside where there were mixed games of rounders or stump cricket, with a soft ball, on the sands. It may surprise American baseball enthusiasts that rounders was counted then by boys as a game for girls. Street games for girls were limited to skipping, either singly, or en masse using a long rope, accompanied by the players singing some jingle. They also had mysterious round-games, somewhat esoteric, which they played in school playgounds and which boys rarely understood. Girl children gave up, or were forbidden to play, street games at a much earlier age than boys; do doubt because they matured much earlier than boys.

18: A Cullercoats fishwife in 1901 (see p. 35).

CHAPTER SEVEN

Disease and Death

During my boyhood, children became aware of disease and death at a much earlier age than they do now, because disease and early death were much more prevalent eight decades ago. Persons· who can call themselves Victorians must be octogenarians or older, and are likely to be the tough members of their families, as death in infancy, youth, or middle-age, was accepted as nothing exceptional, however much regretted. Most families were large ones, and it was a very fortunate one if all children survived to become adults, because many weaker ones succumbed to childish ailments which now can be cured in a matter of days, or prevented by prophylactic measures. Our family was fortunate, as only the first-born died in early babyhood, and the remainder lived to ripe age, having been carefully nursed through the usual children's complaints of whooping cough, measles, various fevers, and septic throats, and were well fed by our parents, who conveyed no inherited physical weaknesses.

Families were large for two reasons; the first because few parents, except male or female rakes, knew anything about contraception, and if they did would have counted birth control as something sinful. The second reason, which applied to poor folk, was to try to ensure that some children would survive to care for their parents in old age, and, from the age they could earn money, contribute to the family income. In those early days there were few pensions for those unable to work because of frailty or old age, except in some professions, the civil service, or the armed forces. The first "old age pension" (Lloyd George's dole) was introduced only in 1908.

If persons were ill, they were almost invariably nursed at home and attended by a general medical practitioner, if they could afford to pay one. It is just and agreeable to record that ethical standards of the average G.P. were very high, and many of them treated the poor without expecting fees, trusting that they could earn enough from their richer patients to obtain a livelihood.

There were infirmaries administered by local authorities or charitable institutions for the needy poor, but even in the former some contribution assessed by the lady almoner was expected from patients who could afford payment. There were also a few isolation hospitals for those contracting infectious diseases, administered by public health authorities, to deter the spread of epidemics, but many children with one or more of these plagues were nursed at home with some primitive means of isolation from the rest of the family. Being admitted to any sort of hospital except for physical injuries carried some stigma about it, and people whispered and spoke with bated breath if one of the family, or a friend, "had to go into hospital". There was reason for this, because in those days illnesses which now can be cured easily and quickly with modern medicine were killers, especially of children.

Doctors, never called medical practitioners then, were prominent and highly respected persons in the community, with an aura of gravity, mystery, and high status about them, along with their morning dress, frock coats, and top hats. So high was the status of many of them that lower-class people bowed or curtsied to them, as they entered the homes of their patients.

There were two main types of doctors; the first, fortunately more numerous, were kindly men with sympathetic bedside manners, and were the repositories of family troubles, and advisers on all sorts of problems unconnected with medicine. The second class were stern and forbidding in manner, mimicking the renowned Dr. Abernethy, Professor of Anatomy and Surgery in the Royal College of Surgeons, who became more renowned, more popular, and richer, the more he insulted his patients. The severe, harsh pronouncements and instructions to patients and their relatives, delivered in a loud voice, led them to believe the doctor was a very wise individual, and his orders were as "laws of the prophets".

The majority of general practitioners became expert diagnosticians of common complaints because of the numerous cases they encountered, though they had few aids to diagnosis and investigation such as X-rays, pathological specimens, etc., so obligatory at the present time. Their tools of their trade, and their types of medicines, were also limited, and chloroform or laughing gas were their simple anaesthetics, only used in extreme cases. Retired

68

doctor friends of mine who remember those days confess that their knowledge of more obscure complaints and methods of treatment were limited. One wonders how many cases of appendicitis were dismissed as "belly ache", and treated as such, till the patients died of peritonitis. The removal of an appendix was counted as a very major operation till 1902, when King Edward VII had his successfully removed. Now it is counted as a minor operation.

In my boyhood days, "kitchen table surgery" was common, as this avoided paying for a bed in hospital, and subsequent nursing was done by members of the patient's family. Thousands of fractures of the limbs were reduced, with or without anaesthetics; thousands of children had their tonsils removed; and even more thousands of boys as babies lost their foreskins, on kitchen tables. In those days most people thought that a lad could never get a proper start in life till circumcised, and interested friends of the family would tenderly enquire if baby had had his little operation yet. No-one was crude enough to use the proper name for this operation.

In addition to their household duties, which were never ending, most mothers of families had to tend the sick, because at frequent intervals one or more of her children would be suffering from some mild or serious complaint. All the children in our family ran the full gamut of chickenpox, measles (German or otherwise), scarlet fever, and acute tonsilitis, but thankfully none of us caught diphtheria, as this was a killing disease in those days, and none of us was consumptive; otherwise we might not have lived beyond childhood. I remember when I joined the army, at the age of seventeen, the medical officer asked if I had suffered from the list of diseases enumerated above, and when I declared I had had all of them, exclaimed: "Fine, you will be a very fit recruit, as you have already been self-inoculated and vaccinated against most infections."

If one of us caught an infectious disease we were immured in the small bedroom, with a bed sheet dipped in carbolic hung over the doorway. Though the others were forbidden to enter the sick-room, we usually caught the disease in turn. I remember, when just an infant without much comprehension, running into the room when the doctor entered it, much to Mother's dismay. However, the doctor laughed and said: "You may as well let him in and out, as he will be certain to catch the complaint whatever you do". My elder brother, Alex, spent six weeks isolated in that bedroom, and nearly went mad with boredom, as he had an active brain; but fortunately a lad of the same age was isolated in a similar bedroom next door, and by leaning out of the window, they were able to converse and exchange books. Recently, many decades later, Alex declared, "I really began my education at that time because the books I received were splendid adventure classics which opened my eyes to a new world".

The epidemic diseases carried off many young children. Some children in my school had no footwear and came to school bare-footed, even in winter, and their schoolfriends soon became acquainted with the words "death" and "dying". I can remember that when I was in junior school it was not unusual for the teacher to announce that "Little Jimmy so and so", who had been absent for some days, would not be coming back to school as he had "gone to Heaven", so his empty place in class could be given to another pupil.

On the whole, we were healthier than most families, and suffered less, because Mother had several specific remedies or prophylactic measures always ready for use. Towards the end of winter she prepared what she called "spring medicine" in large quantities. It consisted of lemon juice and sugar in water with something akin to Epsom salts dissolved in it, and we were urged to drink some, as much and as often as we cared to. As it was quite a pleasant thirst quencher, we did so, and Mother said it would "clear our blood" – it certainly cleared our bowels.

If Mother thought we were "not ourselves", ill-tempered on rising in the morning, having, according to the current phrase, "got out of bed on the wrong side", she administered some Gregory's Powder (called that because a doctor of that name had invented it). I now know the ingredients, which are rhubarb, magnesium, and powdered ginger, with a little cinnamon added. It looked like lumpy cocoa when a quantity was mixed with a little milk in a saucer, before administration by mouth. It tasted foul and gritty, and young patients were often in tears before swallowing the saucerful. We were usually cured from "not being ourselves" with one dose; mainly, I think, for fear of receiving another.

Fenning's Fever Cure, which can still be obtained from old-fashioned chemists, was always kept in Mother's kitchen cupboard, for dosing those with severe colds and high temperatures. It tasted

70

19: A group of children round a barrel-organ at Sandgate in about 1890.

20: 'Paddy's Market', near The Quayside, Newcastle, c. 1900. The children have bowling hoops (see p. 64).

foul and acrid, as it contained, amongst other ingredients, nitric acid, and was given in small doses with a lump of sugar to help the medicine go down! I have never come across any other such nostrum, which could bring a patient into a copious sweat and bring down the temperature, and quell feverish symptoms, if the complaint was of a simple nature. If we had sore throats, Mother tied large, used stockings, preferably sweaty ones, about our necks; and they were surprisingly comforting and efficacious.

In the season of coughs and colds, Mother had made up her special cough mixture by boiling up, all together, a handful of linseed, liquorice, and aniseed balls, then added a little ipecacuanha obtained from the chemist. When complete, the nostrum had the consistency of thin treacle, and was very slimy, which made it revolting to many members of the family, though I found it palatable and a balm to inflamed tonsils and pharynx. If there was the slightest signs of chestiness, our chests were rubbed with camphorated oil or goose grease and covered with wrappings of real flannel not flannelette. On one occasion, when Father was suffering from severe bronchitis, a friend presented him with a bottle of whisky; but so strict were Mother's teetotal tenets that she would not permit him to drink any, but used it instead of camphorated oil to rub on his chest, and locked the bottle away as though it was poison. There was another curious remedy used by many families for chest complaints and rheumatism, which could be obtained from an old chemist famous for it. It consisted of a small bottle filled with some mysterious liquid labelled "poison", with instructions that the drug should not be taken but the bottle itself should be rubbed over the affected part. Apparently the thin film of the oily liquid which had the property of oozing through the glass was sufficient to affect a cure.

Teenagers, especially girls, became thin, weak and weary; and if this persisted, it was said they were going into a decline. This was probably due to malnutrition, or incipient consumption, undiagnosed. It was common practice, if children looked delicate or not sufficiently robust, to feed them with brewers' malt. Though she hated to take it, my sister Eleanor was dosed daily for years, because she was counted as "skinny", but she never put on weight. Actually she had what is now counted as an enviable lissom figure, and rarely had a severe illness till very late in life.

Ringworm was a scourge at the time, common amongst school

children as it was very contagious. Those who contracted it were kept away from school for weeks or months. None of our family caught it because Mother always kept a lump of sulphur which was dabbled in water when our heads were washed. This was done frequently, and our hair carefully combed to discover any nits in it picked up from contact with other school children. Nits and hair lice were so common amongst school children that one of the main duties of school nurses was to examine everyone's head and see that they had proper treatment if necessary. Those with many parasites and ringworm had their heads shaved bare, and washed in carbolic or some other unguent. One of the many plagues of soldiers during the First World War was lice in hair and clothing which tormented their hosts and caused Trench Fever. My brother, Alex, then a professor of entomology, studied the problem of the prevalence of these parasites and came to the conclusion that many civilians recruited into the army brought them with them from England. DDT, which eventually almost exterminated the parasites when it was discovered, was unknown then, so the treatment had to be more radical.

Dental hygiene was almost unknown to the poorer classes of society, so dental diseases were very common, especially amongst school children, and it was quite common to see pupils sitting in class with swollen faces bound up with scarves and allowed to sit near the fire or radiator by sympathetic teachers. Very few authorities provided school dentists to diagnose and treat children, so many suffered abominably, and some deaths could be attributed to septicaemia of the mouth and associated parts. Infants suffering pain when teething were given "teething powders" which were sold in great quantities by chemists. They contained some derivative of opium and they certainly relieved the parents for a time, as the child was put to sleep, but they certainly did not cure the pain. Grandmothers using a silver thimble used to rub the inflamed gums over an erupting tooth, as they supposed there was some magic in silver; but the real effect was to abrade the tissues, allowing the tooth to erupt more easily. They also used the thimble to file down sharp edges of decayed teeth, and plugged cavities in them with cotton wool or bread dough dipped in various liquids such as vinegar, turpentine, tincture of myrrh, or oil of cloves. Most of these were useless, except the last, because the patient needed the services of a dentist, but toothache was often counted as a necessary evil of childhood, and skilled dental treatment was too expensive. However, most chemists were prepared to extract teeth at a shilling a time, and the operations were done with the patient sitting on a stool behind the drug counter.

I was particularly subject to toothache, and in desperation my parents decided to call in a qualified dental surgeon, who came accompanied by our family doctor. I was placed on Mother's bed, anaesthetised with chloroform, and lost most of my milk teeth at one operation. Other members of the family had the same treatment at intervals, as most had soft teeth, and some were almost edentulous by the time they were adults.

Bumps on the head were treated with a copious smear of butter, a penny placed on top of it, and a bandage to keep it in place, and were soon forgotten. Mouldy cheese was often used for dressing cuts and was often very effective, as it has some analogy to the modern penicillin. Cobwebs were sometimes used to dress open wounds, and frequently very successfully, because they had some analogy to fibrin, which is formed in blood clots, by nature, in healing.

Warts on the hands and corns on the feet were common to many people, and every family had some favourite remedy for them, usually made from herbs such as stinging nettles. Young folk used them, repeating some incantation or supposed spell as they were applied, such as: "Warts, warts, go away, don't come back another day." Boils and abscesses were treated with cupping glasses which were in the shape of Chinese teacups. They were heated in hot water and inverted over the offending place. As they cooled, a partial vacuum formed inside them, and this had the effect of drawing out septic matter and the core of a boil. Doctors possessed specially manufactured cupping glasses, but patients who could not afford their fees used any convenient small bottles. Some doctors still used live leeches for blood-letting, as they have been used for centuries, and it was not unusual to hear an unpopular practitioner referred to as a "leech".

CHAPTER EIGHT

Infant Schooling

My schooling began at the early age of three, and now at the age of eighty-eight, I feel my education is far from complete. There were few nursery schools at the beginning of the century, but some schools administered by local authorities were prepared to take toddlers into a baby class providing that they were properly weaned and toilet trained. I was escorted to and from Chillingham Road'infants' School by my sister, Edith, and I was told later that Mother was in tears when I started off with her on my first day.

Coming from a 'respectable' family, and being a rather timid and retiring child, I found it difficult at first to associate with more robust and turbulent pupils coming from less orderly homes, who spoke in extreme Geordie dialect, so I dwelt on the words of my school teacher, which I could understand, and gained her approbation as a 'bright pupil'. This view of my ability only lasted till I went to the junior school, came up against cleverer children, and became just one of the majority.

I remember little about early school days except the games we played in the school yard, and two incidents, both a little embarrassing. The first was that, when aged five, I was made to take part in a school concert dressed as a policeman, holding up a mock motor car for speeding – motor cars were just appearing on roads at that time and were things of wonder. The vehicle was represented by four kneeling children twirling open Japanese sunshades, simulating wheels, with two other actors sitting on stools as driver and passenger. I had an unfortunate accident shortly before my entrance on to the stage because of nerves and being too shy to ask to go to the toilet, so had to be quickly dried and re-dressed before playing my part. The second incident, still fresh in my mind, was the visit of a Japanese gentleman, an educationalist, visiting the school. As I had some ability to remember verse, I was chosen to recite a piece which began 'Twas

1 and 22: Fisherfolk at Newbiggin-by-the-Sea where the author was taken for a week's
holiday as a small child.

the night before Christmas, and all through the house, not a creature was stirring, not even a mouse'.

When I had finished, the eastern gentleman, grinning expansively, presented me with a child's story book in which he had written on the flyleaf an inscription in Japanese. Neither he nor anyone else translated it into English, and though I kept this souvenir for many years, the inscription remained an enigma.

Oddly enough, the next Japanese man I came into contact with, many years later, was during the attack on Singapore, and he threw a hand grenade at me.

Of all the members of the teaching staff who endeavoured to teach me at elementary schools, the only one I can recall distinctly was the drill sergeant, Paddy O'Toole. There were no teachers with specialised training in physical education in ordinary schools, but occasionally our class teacher made us stand up and perform some simple arm exercises, mainly to take the fidgets out of us, so Paddy O'Toole's visits were a welcome change. He appeared at intervals of two or three weeks, as his duties took him to several schools. He was a typical old soldier, from a regular regiment, and probably had been a P.T. sergeant. He was always dressed in a tunic and trousers, almost identical with that of military patrol uniform, wearing a navy blue forage cap and carrying a silver-topped sergeant's staff. He took several classes at a time into the playground and taught us how to stand to attention and march round in military fashion, and form up in spaced lines to perform knees bend, trunk turning, etc., similar to the current exercises for soldiers. He never took his tunic or cap off when teaching these, as he was getting on in years and could have done with a fugleman, which is the name for a trained soldier, assistant to a drill NCO, who demonstrates movements to recruits. Though he could be, or pretend to be, stern, he was a kindly man and made no fuss about being addressed as Paddy by the children. I thought a lot of him, as I did about anyone wearing a uniform.

When I progressed to a senior elementary school, showing no brilliance in my scholastic subjects but liking Geography and History, I was made to sit a scholarship examination with the object of receiving higher education at Rutherford College, similar to that provided in grammar schools, but without their long traditions. I was not awarded a scholarship, and no-one would have been more surprised than myself if I had been, judging by the answers I gave in arithmetic and other subjects. Fortunately, the authorities decided to interview some unsuccessful candidates who might warrant assisted scholarship, which meant that parents should pay half fees. For the English papers, candidates had been asked to invent and write a story featuring the seaside, and apparently mine had an unusual twist which attracted the attention of the examiners; so despite poor showing in other subjects, I was awarded an assisted scholarship. Strange how one tiny piece of writing could influence the course of my life, because without it, perhaps, I would never have received any higher education, due to my parents' inability to pay full fees.

There is more about Rutherford College in the last chapter of this book. I spent the last years of my boyhood days there, and though still a youngster, entered manhood within a few weeks of leaving school.

CHAPTER NINE

Holidays and Treats

Few parents in our stratum of society could afford to take their children away for holidays, so they had to be content with an occasional day at the seaside; fortunately not far from Newcastle, so a cheap train ride could be taken to Tynemouth, Whitley Bay or Cullercoats. I can remember only one longer visit to the seaside as an infant, when Mother took the five children to Newbiggin-by-the-Sea for a week. We stayed with a Mrs Thompson who took in lodgers, and, looking back, I feel that it must have been a great burden for Mother looking after us in a house, not her own, and supervising our activities on the beach so that we were preserved from drowning in the North Sea, which is rarely calm and benign. I was too young at the time to remember much about the holiday except that it rained and blew most of the time, and our bedrooms were filled with drying clothes, and sand, seaweed, and other odiferous collections of marine life picked up on the beach to be taken home as souvenirs.

When I was a little older, about thirteen years of age, we began to take holidays of a different sort, and I remember them with nostalgia now. This was due to the enterprise of our elder brother, Alex, who was now an adult, and who rented a farm labourer's cottage for five pounds a year in an isolated hamlet situated in south Northumberland. The hamlet consisted of a farmhouse with a large farm-yard, barn and cow-byre, and eight tiny dwellings adjacent to it. Our cottage had three rooms, one on top of the other, the ground floor one was both kitchen and living-room and had a closed stairway leading to the bedroom above. The top room, in the eaves, was another bedroom, reached by open stairs from the first, so those sleeping in the latter had little privacy. There was no running water laid on, and it had to be collected from a pump in the farm-yard. The privies, with dry earth closet, were not very private, and situated thirty yards away, near the hedge of a field. Though the accommodation was rough, I enjoyed the holidays in that hamlet cottage more than any in my whole life.

That hamlet was, and still is, situated ten miles from any railway station, so we had to walk that distance going to and from it. If we could afford the fare of one shilling and sixpence, which was seldom, we could ride in the postman's trap, which made one journey a day from and to the nearest railhead. The postman was a surly sort of chap, and though he liked to take fares, he disliked any passengers; and several times during a trip would remark "Ha ye no mercy on me horse? Git doon and walk up this hill", though he remained in the vehicle himself. Travelling with the conveyance was often more exhausting than doing the journey on foot. I can recall few rides in the trap, since no-one thought that it was any particular hardship for a boy of nine to walk the ten miles, for even younger children from the hamlet walked this distance to and from school every day.

Within a few yards were the heather-clad fells and grouse moors, and only a pasture separated us from the beautiful river, a tributary of the Tyne. What more could a boy want? The fells were open to us, and there was the occasional chance in the grouse season of earning a few pence acting as a junior beater. The fields and woods nearby were full of wild-life, and we could play at being Robin Hoods. The river was a constant pleasure, rarely visited by anglers so we had it to ourselves. Patrick, a lad of my own age and son of the farmer, and I, spent whole days playing on or about it, only driven back to our homes by our stomachs and boyish appetites. The water gurgled over rocks and stones, as it was still a mountain stream, but there was one large pool on which we floated a home-made raft made from timber filched from the barn. Like most home-made rafts, it was an unstable craft and we rarely used it without getting drenched or falling overboard. Fortunately, our thick woollen clothing retained its warmth, so however wet we got, we never caught cold.

In times of spate, we set night lines to catch fish, but if we did catch any we threw them back, for fear the water bailiff would discover that we had been poaching, and prevent us from playing by the river.

Watching, and occasionally taking part in, the never-ending work on the farm, was a constant joy to me, and I counted it a great privilege to help drive the cows to and from the fields; taking

23: The Jesmond Vale 'Hoppings' in 1914 (see p. 95).

the horses to be shod some miles away; chopping down the tall thistles which sprang up in the pastures; and cutting bracken for beasts bedding on the open fellsides. Haymaking time was best of all because everyone was welcome to help, even quite young children. Small farmers such as the one in our hamlet had few mechanical aids to harvesting except a horse-drawn reaper, and this could only be used in large fields – the grass in smaller ones was cut with scythes and laid in parallel swathes to dry. These swathes, when dry on top, had to be turned by hand, using a large wooden rake. There was a knack in doing this because the swathe had to be kept in one piece and turned with a continual movement of the rake. Watching this being done by an expert was akin to watching a breaker on a sea-shore gradually turning itself from one end to the other before coming to rest on a beach. Haymaking in that part of the country might be a very lengthy operation, as long spells of dry, sunny weather were rare. After the swathes were turned the hay was piled into heaps called kyles, about three feet in height, for further drying. Some days later, several kyles were gathered together to form a loose-cone-shaped stack called a pike. These pikes remained in the fields for several days, and were so skilfully made that rain ran off the surface and did not penetrate the inside; so, given a good fine day, they were ready for transporting to the barn. There were no haywains in that part of Northumberland, and each pike was transported whole, on a flat vehicle with no sides to it, called a bogie. Its floor was only a few inches raised from the ground, and its two wheels were quite small. Moving the pike from the ground onto the vehicle was done by tipping the floor backwards till it rested on the ground, touching the base of the pike, and then placing a chain round the lower part of the hay. The two ends of the chain were attached to a wooden roller at the front end of the vehicle, and this was turned by hand using a stout iron handle with cogwheels at one end. As the chain tightened, the pike was drawn forward onto the bogie and its floor resumed its natural position on the axles parallel to the ground. Riding on top of a pike on a hay bogie, from a hayfield to the farm, gave me such happiness that I still count it as one of the most pleasurable diversions in a long life.

Our holidays and tenancy of that little cottage ended on the outbreak of the First World War, and for many reasons I was unable to revisit that little hamlet until sixty years later, when touring Northumberland by car. To my great joy, it was unchanged, as though time had passed it by. I could find no person about until I entered the barn and stable-yard. There were no signs of any horses, but an elderly man was loading a lorry with timber. Hesitating a little I asked "I wonder if there can be a farmer called R . . . still working here?" The man looked up, smiled a little, and remarked "I'm Patrick; Basil, remember our raft on the river?".

I felt abashed, almost ashamed, that Patrick should recognise me without hesitation, and I had addressed him almost as a stranger. Neither of us had time to reminisce, owing to urgent appointments which had to be kept, but I trust on some future occasion we shall meet again and renew our boyhood friendship.

During the early years of this century few parents in Newcastle could afford to indulge their children by entertainment which cost money, so the youngsters looked forward to several red-letter days in the year which could be enjoyed at small cost or none at all. They were Carling Sunday, Paste Egg Day, Christmas, and New Year's Day. We used to count the Sundays up to Easter, which was Paste Egg Day, by the rhyme:

Tid, Mid, Misere,
Carling, Palm,
and Paste Egg Day.

Carling Sunday in the North East is a curious festival, during which boiled grey peas, called carlings, are eaten in great quantities, mainly by children, from paper bags. Its origins are still debated by local folk lore researchers, but the most likely theory refers to the Civil War, when Newcastle suffered a long siege and the inhabitants were almost starving, till a ship from the Continent broke the blockade in the Tyne bringing a cargo of foodstuffs, mainly grey peas, which filled the bellies of the defenders and enabled them to hold out; thus the motto of the City "Fortifer Defendit Triumphans".

Paste Egg Day was an Easter festival, and the word 'Paste' is a corruption of Pasque, and has a long history. From the beginnings of Christianity, it was customary for persons to present each other with hens' eggs, which were often coloured purple by rubbing the shells with the dull purple flowers of a 'Pasque Flower', a perennial

84

herb related to a buttercup. Before Easter Sunday, mothers of families would hardboil dozens of eggs, adding various items to the water in the pans to colour the shells. Onion skins were favourite, as they produced delicate brown and yellow tints, coffee dregs would produce dark brown, cochineal red, and indigo a beautiful blue. Eggs were cheap in those days, sometimes twenty-six for a shilling, so baskets of the coloured eggs were taken by children to distribute to friends, who would return the compliment. It was not unusual for a child to receive more than half a dozen paste eggs, which were not eaten straight away but used for two pastimes. One was japing or jowping, which meant tapping – a common word amongst miners, communicating with others in the mines by striking the coal face with a blunt instrument. The children's game was to discover who had the hardest egg by striking the pointed end against that held by a friend. In some cases the broken egg was forfeited, and handed over to the owner of that which was unbroken. On Easter Monday, a bank holiday, children were dispatched to parks and open spaces to 'bool' (bowl or roll) their collection of eggs down grassy banks, with the object of ascertaining which would roll farthest without breaking. This having been accomplished, the children, having been provided with some salt, would eat as many as possible. I still marvel at the numbers which could be consumed by robust young boys at one sitting without serious consequences.

I was very happy that my wife for many years still provided paste eggs on Easter Day, until the end of her life, in sufficient quantity for gifts to friends. Unexpectedly receiving one, an old friend, an octogenarian, almost burst into tears, exclaiming: "This is very evocative, reminding me of boyhood – I have not received one for nearly seventy years".

The next red letter day in our lives was that of the Sunday School Treat which generally took place at Whitsuntide. The entertainment consisted of a journey to some suitable field a few miles into the countryside, where games and competitions were held, and picnic food provided. It was organised by the Sunday School teachers, and young men of the church congregation. The latter formed an advance party, taking with them a bell tent, a cast iron boiler, crockery, provender, and a few chairs for the use of adults. There were no motor cars owned by members of the church, and very few to be seen on the roads, so they travelled in a horse-drawn brake starting off an hour or so before the main party. I was always there to see them off from in front of our church, as I always thought there was something romantic about the loading of baggage, which I imagined similar to setting out on a small military expedition. The main party, about forty excited children with teachers in command, rode in two horse charabancs or wagonettes, and as we seldom rode in any conveyance the journey was novel and enjoyable, especially when passers-by and folks standing on the sides of the road returned our cheers.

It was even more exciting when we arrived at the venue and saw the bell tent erected, the iron boiler smoking away, and benches and tables set out in a barn. A field with a barn in it was usually selected, as the weather at Whitsuntide was rarely dry or very salubrious. A sort of haversack ration in a paper bag, consisting of a couple of cheese or ham sandwiches, a jam sandwich, a piece of fruit slab cake, and a large bun with sugary icing on top, was given to each child, with instructions that this was to serve for two meals, picnic lunch and tea. For drink,each child received a bottle of pop, fizzy lemonade, or ice-cream soda; the latter because of its name was counted preferable. A senior member of the church owned a 'pop' factory and provided them free.

After picnic lunch, games were organised – stump cricket for the boys, and rounders for the girls, though more adventurous lads escaped and went birdnesting. This was frowned upon, but not so much as it would be in the present time when preservation of the environment has become obligatory. Boys finding a nest already robbed used an odd word, and pronounced it as 'huggied' (possibly derived from hugger mugger – in confusion).

In mid-afternoon, sports were organised, and my father, being a skilled runner, took these seriously, as he did any pastime, giving advice to the contestants and sometimes brief training, advising eating and drinking sparingly before the races. These were limited to sprints of eighty yards or less, sack races, three-legged races, and crawling for the youngest children. I remember bursting into tears because I did not win a crawling race, having become involved in a cow pat on the course, and being chided by Father, who remarked severely: "If you cannot win a race or a competition in life you must learn to be a good loser."

Modest prizes were distributed to winners, and all losers were entered for a handicap sprint – handicap according to age, which was so carefully contrived that it was difficult to judge who were first past the post, so everyone received a consolation prize of a couple of buns in a bag.

Then came the tea interval followed by packing up for the return journey. The children were then directed to cleaning up the field – picking up all litter – and those who picked up the most received any bags of buns left over from the meals.

We were encouraged to sing songs and catches on the way home, though most of the younger children nodded and fell asleep in the conveyances. Parents received us when we arrived at the church door and hustled us off to our homes and beds, tired but happy. Looking back, I am amazed that a simple pleasure like the Sunday School Treat could give such happiness, and I trust the organisers have had their reward in heaven.

In the North East of England, Christmas and New Year's Day are celebrated almost equally. The first, quite rightly, is mainly children's day, and the second a festival for older persons, who begin celebrating it on New Year's Eve.

I wish I could regain that childish excitement and pleasurable anticipation at the approach of Christmas that I and other children experienced then. Except on birthdays and Christmas Day, one seldom received presents, except perhaps some odd tips of a few pence from well-off callers at our home. These were so rare that I still remember the donors. One, on handing over sixpence, admonished me to "spend that judiciously" and the other, my Uncle Archie, an old soldier, who could ill afford giving anyone sixpence, saying heartily: "Now, lad, do what you like with this, no nonsense about money boxes, but spend it prodigally". I did not know the word 'prodigally' but understood his meaning.

The harbinger of Christmas was the arrival of a dead turkey, usually carried into the house by Father who was able to obtain one from a friend in the poultry business at a cheap rate. The bird was unplucked, with all its feathers on, and all its viscera inside it, so it looked immense. Mother started to pluck it immediately, and the children were allowed to help her. When this was complete, there were scores of pieces of quills still attached to the skin, so these were burnt off with a lighted taper made of newspapers, filling the house with the acrid smell of burnt feathers. Mother disembowelled the bird in private, as this was counted a distasteful sight for young eyes, then put it on a larder shelf for everyone to

24: Bigg Market in about 1895 (see p. 112).

25: Bigg Market in about 1910.

view and admire. It was placed next to the Christmas pudding, already partly cooked in a cloth bag tied tightly at the top ready for another two hours' cooking on Christmas morning. Everyone had helped to stir the mixture of flour, suet, sultanas, currants, and candied peel, and knew that Mother had added a threepenny piece which some lucky person at the table would find in his portion.

To me, the time between teatime and bedtime on Christmas Eve was interminable, only relieved by the groups of carol singers who sang in the street. My elder brothers and sisters were usually amongst a group of singers from our church, but I was too young to participate. At last nine o'clock came, and I needed no persuasion to go upstairs to bed.

Everyone in our house hung up stockings on bedrails, expecting them to be filled by Christmas morning. We children knew what to expect in them – an orange, an apple, a twopenny toy, a sixpence, some imitation coins in gold paper, a small bar of Fry's Cream Chocolate, and a sugar mouse or pie. We hoped for, and generally received, another present too large to fit inside a stocking, something we had yearned for, but were sometimes disappointed that it was only a pencil box, the sort of container for school children's equipment which is almost impossible to buy nowadays. It was made of polished wood with an upper and lower compartment on a pivot at one end. The top compartment was grooved to hold pens and pencils and the lower one partitioned to hold India rubbers, a pencil, a pencil-sharpener, and pen nibs. The top had a ruler recessed in the wood which could be slid out for use. The only pleasure this utility present afforded was when it happened to be more decorative than those belonging to other school children.

As the baby of a large family, I was probably more fortunate than the rest of the children, receiving more expensive presents which could not be put into a stocking, and I still recall the Christmas morning when, to my delight but not surprise, I received a rocking-horse. I had seen it several times in a shop close to my father's place of business, at the age of four, and was so enamoured of it that I believed I already possessed it, repeatedly referring to it as 'my Dobbin'. That Christmas morning, I was awake long before the rest of the family, and alarmed that in my bedroom was only my filled stocking on the bedrail, so I went into my mother's room, woke her, and almost in tears asked "Where is my Dobbin?" She shushed me for disturbing the household and Father awoke and exclaimed: "For goodness sake and peace, go downstairs and look in the passage." I scrambled down, and there in shadow stood the rocking horse, my Dobbin.

Its body was covered with hide, it had a removable saddle and harness and stirrups, and a real tail of horse-hair. I mounted it immediately and started to rock, and persisted in doing so for several days, except at meals. Some friend, the next day, presented me with a tin sword, and, much to Mother's distress, I waved it about, mounted, charging imaginary enemies, thus inducing in myself a proclivity for martial activities which has lasted me all my life. Dobbin must have cost a great deal more than my parents could easily afford, and years later when it was given away, having become a mangy nuisance, Mother remarked "That did cost a pretty penny, but you had o set your heart on it in the shop that we thought you might have a fit or convulsions and spoil our Christmas if we did not buy it."

Our Christmas dinners of turkey and plum pudding are particularly memorable, because it was the only time in the year when folk of our social class dined on turkey or any fowl. Nowadays, turkey meat is always available all the year round, sometimes cheaper than beef, so it is no longer a luxury. We never had a Christmas tree in our house, but what we called 'a mistletoe bough' made from two wooden sticks set at right angles to each other and covered with paper and tinsel, holly, and a piece of mistletoe hanging down to encourage kissing under it. Mother always kept from Christmas to Christmas lots of paper-chains and Chinese lanterns which could then be bought very cheaply, and the girls decorated the whole house till it looked like a bower, and was a potential fire risk because of gas illumination.

Christmas Day itself was not a day for parties, as many folk preserved it as a solely religious festival, but Boxing Day was one for enjoyment. For many years in my early life we were invited to tea and supper at the home of a family who lived at the other side of the city. They were looked upon as our rich friends, because they lived in a house with three storeys plus basement and attics, and usually employed two maids. Their family was analogous to ours – six children of about the same ages as ourselves. The journey to visit them was an adventure in itself, because I travelled with

Mother and the girls in a hackney horse cab, since trams were few or not running on the holiday. Father and the boys walked three miles there and back. One of my most vivid memories is of a journey in a cab when five years old, during a snowstorm, and even at that age I felt sorry for the cabman wrapped up in an overcoat and cape, being covered in snow, and the poor scraggy horse slowly clip-clopping through the frozen streets; and both of them having to work on Boxing Day.

On arrival at what we thought was a mansion, the adults gathered in the drawing-room which was on the first floor, and the children – twelve of us – spread ourselves over the rest of the house playing games suitable to our various ages. The older lads played billiards on a half-sized table, an expensive piece of furniture; the girls gossiped in bedrooms, and the youngest children played hide and seek. There was a service lift between the basement kitchen and the dining room on the ground floor, and I, as the youngest and smallest, was placed in it, and in a mixture of terror and daring, transferred up or down. I never remember the return journeys home, as I slept solidly in the cab after a surfeit of good food and ginger pop.

Between Christmas and New Year, and, sometimes before the advent of the festive season, groups of 'guizers', akin to the mummers, in other parts of England, called at houses with or without permission to act a little playlet and collect a few coppers as largess.

The players were usually youngsters in their early teens, though in the past guizers were usually adults. They preferably selected houses in which parties were being held, where their performance would add interest to the gaiety, and amuse the company with the remnants of some curious rite handed down from generation to generation, and in that time some words have been forgotten or lost their original meaning. The troop consisted of a leading player called Number 1, and another leader called King George; a player called Dr Brown; a boy dressed as a tatty woman called Betty Funny; plus a chorus of boys. They were dressed in what they imagined was medieval costume with swords, and King George wore a crown and something representing armour. Having received permission to enter the house and give their performance the playlet began with the entrance of Number 1 who pronounced as follows:-

No.1 I lift the sneck and enter in
Hoping a battle will soon begin;
Stir up the fire and make a light
For in this house there'll be a fight.
If you don't believe the words I say
Step in King George, and clear the way.

Enter King George and chorus

King G. Here comes King George;
King George is my name,
With sword and pistol by my side
I hope to win the game.

No.1 The game, sir?

King G. The game, sir, lies in my power
I'll cut him into mincemeat
In less than half an hour.

No.1 Who, sir?

King G. I, sir, take your sword and try, sir.

King George and No.1 fight with swords and No.1 falls dead.

King G. Oh! dear, Oh! dear, what have I done;
I've killed my father's other son,
Send for the fivepenny doctor!

Chorus There ain't no fivepenny doctor.

King G. Then send for the tenpenny one.

Enter Dr Brown carrying bag, etc., and dressed in morning coat and top hat.

Chorus Here comes Dr. Brown
The best old doctor in the town.

King G. What made you the best doctor in the town?

Dr.B. My travels, sir.

King G. How far did you travel?

Dr.B. England, Ireland and Scotland and Wales,
And back to England once again.

King G. What can you cure?

Dr.B. A dead man alive.
I've got a little bottle
In my big inside pocket
That says 'Nicky nack rise up'.

Dr. B. administers a drop from the bottle.

Dr. B. Rise up, dead Dick.

No.1 does so.

No.1   Once I was dead,
         But now I'm alive.
         God bless the doctor
         That made me alive.

King G.   My brother's come to life again;
            We'll never fight no more;
            We'll be as kind as brothers
            As we never were before.

Enter Betty Funny.

Betty F.   Here comes Betty Funny
             I'm the man that carries the money.
             If you haven't got silver,
             Copper will do.
             If you haven't got copper, God bless you.
             Put your hand in your pocket,
             And pull out your purse,
             A penny or tuppence will do you no worse.

Betty takes up a collection from the audience with comical gestures.

All the players   Pockets full of money
                    Barrels full of beer,
                    We wish you a merry Christmas,
                    and a happy New year.
                    Good night to you all, good night.

Exit.

New Year in Newcastle was celebrated as fervently as Hogmanay in Scotland, though it was never referred to by that name. Mother and Father always attended the Watch Night Service on New Year's Eve at our church, and then returned home to receive 'First Footers' who were usually members of the congregation, and came to wish us good fortune for the coming year, shortly after midnight on the Eve. It was obligatory – Mother insisted on this – that the first person to step into the house was dark-haired, as a fair-haired person might bring bad luck. It was also obligatory that he or she brought a piece of coal, piece of wood, a silver coin, and a piece of cake or bread to ensure that the household would never be without heat, kindling, money and food during the coming year. The visitors were entertained with sandwiches, cake and Mother's home-made wine. Other households visited would provide whisky or sherry, but in our teetotal home these were taboo. However, Mother's home-made dandelion or ginger wine was just as alcoholic. The visitors would not stay long, but departed after the refreshment to call at several other homes and did not return to their own till almost breakfast time on New Year's Day. Some First Footers might be entire strangers but were never turned away from a door as this was inhospitable and might bring ill luck.

One event during the year to which every child looked forward with pleasurable anticipation was 'The Hoppings' held on the Town Moor each June at the same time as the horse racing at Gosforth Park. 'Hoppings' is a North Country term for a fair with roundabouts, coconut shies, side-shows,etc. The official name for the festivities was the Temperance Festival, which was organised by persons advocating non-alcoholic beverages in an effort to attract families away from the race meeting where there was much drinking and drunkenness.

In addition to the delights of riding on huge wooden horses on roundabouts, sliding down a tower on a mat, and having goes on 'the shuggy shoes' – large swings with gondola-like seats – which the passengers operated by pulling on ropes, there was the added treat of being able to buy strawberries at tuppence per bag, or squashy ones at one penny.

Adjacent to the fairground was an athletic meeting, and a Military Tournament provided by the soldiers of the local garrison. Father was one of the organisers, so we always got good seats for the tournament, and I was an avid spectator, watching the military drill, tent pegging and mock combats on horseback, and a musical ride by lancers, which added further to my addiction for military pursuits.

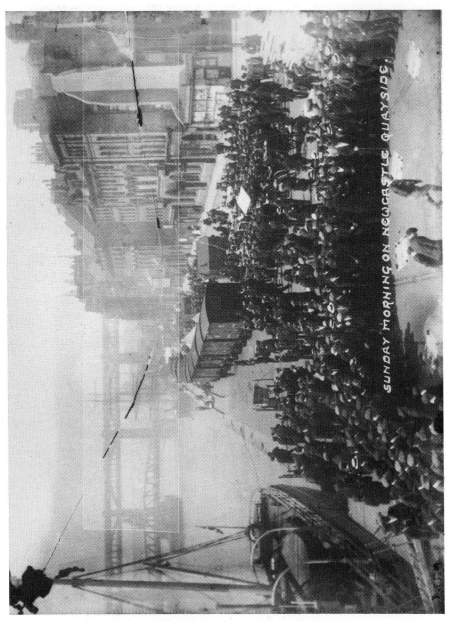

SUNDAY MORNING ON NEWCASTLE QUAYSIDE.

26: The 'rough and rowdy' Quayside Sunday market in about 1900 (see p. 113).

27: The Quayside market in about 1915.

CHAPTER TEN

Family Diversions

In Edwardian times, before there were cinemas, radio, or television, which now provide entertainment on tap, most people had to provide their own amusement as cheaply as possible. Naturally no member of our family, even if adult, ever frequented public houses, but amused themselves at home with hobbies, simple games, and reading. We were not a musical family and none of us had much talent for playing an instrument, which is a pity, because few of us appreciated good music till late in life. I was about eight years old before we possessed a piano, and its arrival was a great event. To have a piano in one's parlour was looked upon as a step towards gentility, and commented upon by friends and neighbours. It was quite common to hear a tart, envious remark such as "Do you know that they have bought a piano, and one of the girls is to have lessons – they must be getting on in the world – I hope they are not getting too big for their boots". Even the possession of that new invention, a gramophone, was looked upon with envy and certainly our family never possessed one.

It was my mother who eventually determined to own a piano because her own parents had possessed one and she thought such an instrument would complete her ménage. Father was not so enthusiastic, mainly because of the expense, so Mother said she would buy one from her own money, and the instrument was always known as 'Mother's piano'.

To buy anything except a piano on hire purchase in those days was thought 'de trop' by middle class folk, but the poor paid their few pennies a week to Scots Drapers, as tally men were called. Mother paid off what was owing on the piano so quickly that she might just as well have paid cash, and announced proudly: "It's mine now", and sat down and played a few notes of 'The Keel Row'. My sisters had some music lessons but never got very far beyond 'The Fairy Land Waltz', and a few exercises, so when a musical evening was organised we depended on the services of more skilled musicians amongst our circle of friends. Our repertoire was usually selected from a collection of traditional ballads such as "Come into the Garden, Maud", "Just a Song at Twilight", "When you Come to the End of a Perfect Day, etc.; Gilbert and Sullivan, especially "Take a Pair of Sparkling Eyes"; the "Indian Love Lyrics"; and jolly songs from The Scottish and British Students' Song Books. Recently two of them: "Mud, Mud, Glorious Mud and "Medicinal Compounda" have been resuscitated by modern entertainers. What are now looked upon as terribly jingoistic ditties, tunes of glory, were very popular, such as "We don't want to fight, but by jingo, if we do, we've got the ships, we've got the men and got the money too", "Hearts of Oak", etc. Sentimental songs such as 'Tom Bowling the Darling of our Crew' used to reduce me to childish tears. Sisters Eleanor and Edith both had good voices and were fond of "Pale Hands I Loved beside the Shalimar" and "I'll Sing you Songs of Araby and Tales of Far Kashmir; but unfortunately they were a little shy and rarely finished them because of stage fright in front of company. Father was tone deaf, but was a great reciter of verse. One of his great recitations was "Barbara Fletchic" – 'Up from the valleys rich with corn', etc., and did it very well. Musical evenings usually terminated with "ohn Brown's Body", missing out successive words in the chorus, each time replacing them with "um" or a grunt, till only "John was left; but we finished with a triumphant: "his soul goes marching on".

When our family gave children's parties, which was seldom, we started with formal games, usually supervised by Father, who liked us to play them with much thought and seriously, without too much frivolity and loud laughter, till he got tired and left us to our own devices. His favourite was "Subject and Object", later transmogrified into "Twenty Questions" on the B.B.C. Our method of playing was to send two members of the company outside the parlour door while they decided on who was subject and who was object – such as "a minister and his pulpit". They then entered the room again, and were quizzed to discover what they represented. If this was not discovered after an agreed number of questions, they had another turn. Father used to appeal to us to think hard instead of asking funny questions, as I feel sure he wished the game to be educational rather than amusing.

'Priest of the Parish' was another game, subject to forfeits if a player was at fault. Forfeits took the place of losing bets of money in those days, the losers being obliged to do something slightly ridiculous in the eyes of the company. The players sat in a ring, and an umpire in the middle allotted each the name of a coloured cap and they had to be addressed as such – Mr. Red Cap, Miss Pink Cap, etc. The umpire standing in the middle began, being careful not to look at any particular player, and announced: "The priest of the parish has lost his considering cap – some say this and some say that but I say Mr. Blue Cap has it". Mr. Blue Cap had to reply promptly: "I, sir, nay, not I, sir." The umpire asked: "Who then, sir?" and Mr. Blue Cap responded: "Some say this, some say that, but I say Mr. White Cap". If he remembered his title, which was often unlikely, Mr. White Cap referred to another person with a different coloured cap and so on. If a player forgot his colour, or was not prompt enough in responding, he was awarded a forfeit, and had to stand on his head in a corner, or crawl round the room imitating a grunting pig, or perform some other absurdity. It was remarkable how few people could last out the game without failing to respond promptly when the game was played fast.

Three kissing games were very popular, especially with the girls. Postman's Knock was very simple. One player outside the parlour door pretending to be the postman knocked, and the players would shout: "Who is the letter for?" The postman, either a boy or a girl, called out a name of one of the opposite sex and the owner went outside and exchanged a fervent kiss or two and took the postman's place to continue the game. The most popular kissing game, which we called either: "Sally sits a-weeping" or "Lay the cushion down", which I believe were two games which we mixed up as one, and played as follows:-

One girl knelt on a cushion in the middle of a circle of the remaining players and pretended to be sobbing her heart out. She was "Sally", and the other players joined hands, and moved round in a circle singing –

Sally sits a-weeping, a-weeping, a-weeping,
She's sighing for her lover, her lover, her lover,
Who has left her all forlorn. [One trusts he had not got her into trouble].

100

Rise, Sally, rise, wipe your weeping eyes
Wipe your weeping eyes – choose to the east
And choose to the west,
The one that you love best.

Sally, holding the cushion, selected a boyfriend and knelt in front of him, and the other players gave advice singing –

The best bed is a feather bed,
The best bed of all;
The best bed is a feather bed,
Not one of pease straw.

And Sally sang distastefully –

The pease straw is dirty,
'Twill dirty all my gown.

Then the company replied –

Never mind, me bonny lass, but lay the cushion down.

Sally then knelt down on her cushion and exchanged kisses with her selected boy-friend, and then the company sang –

Now you are married, we wish you joy;
First the girl and then the boy;
Seven years after seven years over,
Now is the time to kiss and give over.

(It was many years before I realised that the real words were first *a* girl and then *a* boy, and the cushion was a bed on which they conceived.)

In playing "Blind Man's Buff", what fun the girls had pretending to be shy, and avoiding capture, then allowing themselves to be caught if the blind man was attractive, because he was entitled to a kiss.

What rollicking fun we had seeing a blindfolded person trying to pin a tail on to the donkey depicted without one, on a card hanging on the wall, and what enjoyment playing musical chairs; and statues, when every player had to stand stock still whatever

28: The Theatre Royal, Newcastle, in about 1890. Here the author was taken to see Peter Pan when he was twelve – his first visit to a theatre.

position he or she was in when the music stopped, for we were very simple children, and not sophisticated as many modern youngsters are.

Two games we only played in our parents' absence; one was a development of "Hide and Seek", when players hid themselves upstairs in darkness, and one person pretended to be a ghost coming after them. The ghost in a sepulchral voice would announce his position as he or she stealthily approached: "Mother, I'm on the first step, Mother, I'm on the second step" – "now I'm on the top step, now I'm outside the door"; then, with a ghastly shriek as a player was found: "Now I've got you". As the youngest and possibly most sensitive, this game fascinated but terrified me, and I had nightmares after playing it.

The older boys and girls were addicted to playing "Sardines", which had just been invented, in which couples of different sexes hid themselves in close proximity in confined hiding places so that they could indulge in what is now termed as "necking". Unfortunately, I was too young to participate and enjoy it.

We were very fond in our family of singing rounds such as "London's Burning", "Three Blind Mice", and "One man went to mow, went to mow a meadow." These were usually conducted with seriousness by brother Alec. We were also fond of jingles and nonsense songs, for example "The courtiers at the court of King Caractacus have just gone along to ring those charming bells", and as we repeated the jingle, we added all sorts of comic characters to the list of those following this renowned ancient British king taken prisoner by the Romans. I wonder how ancient this jingle is.

We also recited pieces which had no ending but amused us very much. I recall one usually begun by brother Jim who declared he was going to tell a story that began supposedly in a robber's cave –

"It was a dark and stormy night, and the rain came down in torrents, and the brigand chief said unto Antonio, "Tell us a story". Antonio began as follows "It was a dark and stormy night, and the rain came down in torrents, and the brigand chief said unto Antonio, "Antonio tell us a story" and Antonio began as follows "It was a dark and stormy night etc."; so the tale never got told.

As the youngest, and counted for years as the baby, of the family, I was rarely included in the kissing games or those which required intelligence, but I do remember to this day a gentle, charming girl, older than myself and regrettably still a spinster, giving me a kiss because I seemed out of the games and saying I was "a canny little lad". However, if charades were played at parties, particularly at Christmastide, I was dressed up and given a walking-on part. We never played dumb charades, but always invented and acted little plays, mainly composed by brother Alec, who had a talent for writing dialogue. The company was divided into two groups, and one group went out of the parlour and selected a word to be acted by syllables. For instance, the word might be "pirate", and the syllables counted as "pie" and "rate". Alec would invent an incident about Simple Simon, a pieman, selling his wares, then a bailiff coming to collect rates and turning a family out of their home because of non-payment. Then the full word "pirate" would be illustrated by a nautical play about pirates storming a ship and being driven off. I liked this one, as I was dressed as a cabin boy or powder monkey with a dirk at my side. Guided roughly in the action of the play by Alec, performers could often provide more witty dialogue extempore which added to the amusement. We never mentioned the actual syllables or full words in the dialogue, and the audience had to guess them from the actions and innuendoes.

Like many of my generation, we were never allowed to idle, and I have often envied some acquaintances who could do nothing, elegantly, for long periods, without becoming bored. I have sometimes thought that one could only learn this accomplishment at a very expensive private school, followed by classical reading at "Oxbridge", but I am probably mistaken. Idling or even daydreaming was frowned upon in our family and many others similar to ours in the Victorian and Edwardian periods.

Reading the periodicals of the period, especially the advertisements for games and diversions, it seemed they were never intended for amusement only but were additionally educational or instructive. Even the fiction books we read were never entirely for entertainment but pointed out a moral as well as telling a tale. Thus, at quite an early age, we were introduced to the good books, but as a relief we were allowed to read the children's periodical *Chatterbox*, and *The Boys' Own Paper*, for no harm would come to us from the very fine stories in them where good always triumphed in the end and evil was defeated.

Father persistently read the poets and Shakespeare; Mother had

104

no time to read anything except *Home Chat*, one of the first weeklies for women. My sisters wept over *What Katy Did*, *Little Women*, and its sequel *Good Wives*. Alec read Bernard Shaw and became for a period a sort of pink socialist or Fabian, and Jim plodded away at his school books, and those classics allocated as compulsory reading. I used to devour comics in secret, making my acquaintance with Weary Willie and Tired Tim, and other droles. Though they were proscribed literature I also read *The Gem*, and *The Magnet*, making my acquaintance with Billy Bunter, Harry Wharton, Singh and such, and in my mind wandering about Greyfriars School, wishing I could attend such an establishment instead of the forbidding urban building where I was receiving my education.

There was another well-produced boys' periodical entitled *The Captain*, which I delighted to read if someone lent me a copy. I recall that for a coming birthday present I dearly wanted *The Captain Annual*, and broadcast my wish. On my birthday, there on the breakfast table was a large, thick parcel, obviously a book. However, it was not "The Captain", but a very fine volume entitled *A Child's English Literature* which had obviously been bought for my education. It was years before I got over my disappointment and dipped into it. I still have it and find it useful but I would rather have *The Captain Annual* on my bookshelf.

When not reading or studying, everyone in our family had some hobby or other diversion, usually arising from the current craze. Mother's fingers were never idle and she devoted herself to crocheting lace, and tatting, which she did at speed, continuing this until she was an octogenarian and almost blind. Rag matmaking in Edwardian times became a craze, and nearly everyone had a large mat in front of the kitchen fender made from a hessian backing and cut-up bits of any spare cloth or discarded clothing, which were pushed through the sackcloth with a "progger" and knotted. In making, a large framework was necessary which seemed to fill any room in which it was placed. They took weeks to make and all the family was called in to do a little piece at a time. The finished products were worth the labour as they lasted for decades. Mother was also keen on making patchwork quilts out of any odd remnants of cloth, and all beds were covered with them. I still possess one made by Mother over seventy years ago, and am told that these quilts are now in the height of fashion and very costly to buy.

Father's spare time from reading the poets was taken up with writing letters in beautiful copperplate handwriting. The girls did embroidery, making samplers and scrap books, and making up post-card albums. Alec and Jim, following a popular craze at the beginning of this century, took up fretwork, and the house was filled with unstable shelves, brackets and photograph stands, the glue of which either melted or disintegrated. For some years they took up photography, because cheap cameras were being produced. I still possess a five shilling Brownie camera. The negatives were taken on glass plates, and for want of any other dark room were developed in the lavatory. I was once given a small cardboard camera and a few plates for my instruction and amusement, but being forbidden to use the lavatory for developing attempted this in the coal-shed, sitting on top of the coal, which was perhaps the reason why all the negatives came out a jet black. The photography craze came to a sudden end when sister Eleanor took a gulp of what she thought was lemonade, from a lemonade bottle, but turned out to be developing or fixing fluid. Fortunately, it tasted so foul that she swallowed none of it. There was a ping-pong craze, now called table-tennis. Then there was dining-table billiards for those like ourselves who could not afford even the smallest of proper equipment. Most dining tables had a green baize undercover, and this was used as the surface. Six pockets made of strong wire and string network were clamped on to the corners and edges of the table, with wing nuts on the underside. As a substitute for cushions, long strips of webbing about three inches broad were stretched between the pockets and stood three inches above the table surface. Real billiard balls and cues could be used, and when we had chalked baulk spots etc., the table was ready for play, if it was not too violent. A swift hard shot would result in the billiard ball bouncing back from the webbing edges like a stone from a catapult or leaping on to the floor. However, it kept us amused, and prevented us from visiting billiard halls, which were counted as the haunts of wickedness.

We played checkers, attempted chess, ludo and halma and card games, mainly Snap and Happy Families, and when older tried whist, but this never developed into serious games, as my sisters, being so accustomed to childish games, used to ask "Have I to look at my cards?"

106

When I was about ten years of age the craze for diabolo*, coming from the Continent, swept Great Britain, and within weeks the playgrounds were full of children spinning wooden bobbins on a string stretched between two sticks. To be in the fashion I saved up my pocket money for four weeks to buy an outfit for fourpence. The amusement died almost as quickly as it arrived, and now only seems to be performed on stage by skilled music-hall artistes who make diabolo a sort of juggling and ballet spectacle instead of a child's game.

Following a wide and persistent advertising campaign in newspapers and periodicals, the young male population was persuaded to take up body-building to change themselves from weedy drooping individuals into something like pugilists or Japanese wrestlers. Pictures of a gentleman called Mr. Sandow stripped to the waist, showing him with broad shoulders, a highly developed chest, and enormous biceps and a slender waist were to be found in advertisement columns announcing that boys and men could have similar physique if they followed Mr. Sandow's series of exercises, used pieces of equipment recommended, and took cold baths. The equipment was a pair of iron dumb-bells and two Indian clubs. Brother Jim equipped himself as directed, and when he decided to undertake anything, did it seriously, being no dilettante. I could hardly lift the iron dumb-bells or the clubs, but he exercised diligently and one could hear the crashes of the dumb-bells being struck together overhead or behind his back, coming from the bathroom after he had taken his cold bath. Jim always had a robust figure from birth and at the age of eighty-nine still had, so maybe the exercises did little harm and he remained tough enough to take cold baths each morning till only a few years before his death. Exercising with Indian clubs necessitated space, so this was done in the backyard as there was less danger of one slipping from the grip and going through a window.

From quite an early age, I was smitten with what was referred to as "accomplishments" to entertain one's friends. This referred to simple conjuring, ventriloquism, and shadowgraphy; and instructions on how to perform were given in the *Boy's Own Paper*, and I spent hours trying to learn how to palm a coin or a card,

*Diabolo is a game played with a double-coned top made of wood or metal spun upon a string stretched between two sticks held one in each hand. The top is repeatedly thrown into the air and caught again on the string while still spinning.

and throw shadows of my hand and fingers on to a screen in front of a lighted candle. I once manufactured a ventriloquist's dummy's head out of a flat piece of wood with features painted on it, and lips which moved with elastic. This perhaps was my best effort at entertainment, as it was all so amateurish and absurd that spectators had to laugh.

My brother, Alec, reminiscing about early days, remarked: "I often remember your ventriloquial performances, as the dummy always spoke in a voice as though he was being strangled, because you used to try to speak from your stomach, and the performance always finished by the dummy singing 'A man fell off Grey's Monument! And he only did it once. And I don't suppose he'll do it again for months and months and months.' Then you would say 'dolly's tired', and the dummy saying 'Dolly's going to be sick'."

When I made my first visit to London, I was taken to see the famous Lowther Arcade which ran off The Strand, saw a shop selling tin soldiers, and learned the song about "The Little Tin Soldier" with a little tin sword, who was dying for the love of a little toy fairy; and became an addict collecting model and toy soldiers, which hobby remains to this day. Some kindly person presented me with a toy fort made of painted wood, which I garrisoned and played with for hours, then I started making rough models of ancient siege weapons to storm it. Mother never liked these martial activities, or indeed anything to do with soldiering, and though never actually forbidding, used to remark: "Can you not find anything more useful to do than playing at battles?" Poor Mother, she had very soon to put up with all her sons being in soldiers' uniforms and engaged in real battles. Years before the First World War, Alec joined the Volunteers before they were reconstituted as the Territorial Army. Joining the Volunteers was thought a proper manly and laudable thing to do in Victorian and Edwardian times, and Alec enlisted with many university students who formed K Company of the 6th Battalion, the Northumberland Fusiliers. They wore scarlet tunics and sealskin fusilier caps, somewhat similar to guardsmen's bearskin head-dresses. Mother was so opposed to this uniform that he never put it on in the house, but changed at his drill hall.

When I became eleven years of age and went to Rutherford College, my brothers and sisters were all in their late teens, or adults, and the childish games and occupations I have mentioned

29: The Grand Theatre, Byker, in about 1910.

in this chapter fell into abeyance, as we all found other diversions and interests, some of which are related in the following chapter.

CHAPTER ELEVEN

First Adventures

Though most of the suburbanites of Newcastle lived within a couple of miles of the centre of the city, a visit to the centre was counted as something of an expedition when I was a boy, though we could travel there for a penny or twopence on a tram. The expedition was called "gannin doon the toon", and in my early days I went in the company of my father, or elder brother Alec, both of whom made sure that the trip was educational as well as a pleasure.

There were many elegant shops in the city centre, and though we rarely shopped in them I was fascinated by the apparatus which enabled the counter-hands to send money and bills to a central cash desk by a system of overhead wires, transporting little wooden containers by gravity between the counters and the desk. The counter-hand placed the money and the invoice in one of these containers, and put it into a sort of lift which raised it up to a sufficient level so that it whizzed across the shop to the clerk waiting to receive it, who, after giving a receipt and change, if necessary, reversed the process back to the counter. However, these shops sold little within reach of my few pennies of saved-up pocket money, so the markets were much more to my taste, as there a penny could buy lots of desirable toys and gadgets. One could buy goldfish for one penny, a canary for twopence, and even a puppy for sixpence, from scruffy itinerant traders who had no stalls but wandered amongst the shoppers.

The markets were nearly always crowded with customers or sight-seers, and filled with noise as the traders shouted their wares. One of the most exciting experiences during a visit to the market was being weighed in a special "weigh house" which was done on a gigantic pair of brass scales with a long beam, suspended from which was one pan to hold the weights, and the other with a seat for the customer. The cost was one penny for adults and a half-penny for children. Business was always good, with plenty of

111

customers, and the attendant, who had to keep lifting heavy brass weights on and off the scale, had a strenuous occupation. Sometimes, if a customer was a betting man, the attendant would offer to guess his weight. If he guessed right within two pounds, the customer had to pay threepence; if he failed there was no charge. The attendant rarely lost the bets.

On a recent visit to Newcastle, I found the weigh house still flourishing, with a long queue of customers; but sadly the old brass scales had gone, and a more modern weighing machine had been installed. My father was addicted to being weighed, and carefully retained for many years each ticket showing his weight.

There was another interesting place in the market which fascinated me; it was an upstairs café supplying hot pies and peas, and a buxom lady stood at the foot of the stairs exhorting passers-by to "come and get wor famous hot pies and peas hinnies", almost using force to persuade them to enter her establishment. The succulent odour emerging from the café was so intense to me as a boy that I can smell it still, though I was never allowed to enter, as it was thought unsuitable for young children, for some obscure reason.

On market days an open-air market took place on a site near the Town Hall, and was called the Bigg Market – bigg is a certain type of barley – and nearby were two streets named Corn Market and Groat Market. Such markets had taken place there for centuries, and the Bigg Market still takes place, though it has lost much of its character since my boyhood. Then, as well as stalls selling fruit, vegetables, trinkets, cheap cloth, etc., there were itinerant quack doctors dispensing "cure all" nostrums with appropriate amusing patter, and a quack dentist who operated on a cart, removing teeth without the assistance of an anaesthetic, except a big drum which was beaten violently by a black man to drown any groans from the patients. I now feel sure that some of his first patients during a session were assistants who had mingled with the audience, and by sleight of hand the dentist could produce a gory tooth and exhibit it as though just extracted from a mouth without pain. There was always a sarsaparilla* vendor who produced this tasty drink from a large scarlet machine on wheels, so

*Sarsaparilla is produced from several species of smilax, and is a cooling drink like near beer, but seems to have gone out of fashion.

112

big that it could be mistaken for a fire engine, which made the liquid itself more intriguing.

There were also traders with portable ovens, selling roast chestnuts or roast potatoes, and several sea-food stalls providing saucers of cockles and mussels for customers to eat standing at the counter. I was never allowed to sample these comestibles, but permitted to buy a saucerful of hot, succulent, large, boiled, marrowfat peas, from a stall selling nothing else.

The Winlaton Sword Dancers occasionally attended and performed their curious dance to the sound of a tin whistle, ending up with all swords entwined. Then the troupe consisted of old men in costume trying to earn a few coppers, and differed from modern troupes who sometimes appear on television.

There was yet another market, whose origins were lost in antiquity, held on Sunday mornings on the quayside, but though anxious to, I was never allowed to visit it when a boy as it was rough and rowdy, and Sabbath Day trading was frowned upon by my parents. Newcastle quayside on the coaly Tyne was then a most fascinating place for small boys such as myself, and when I was taken to visit it on non-market days I was enthralled by its atmosphere and the persons who worked there. In the early nineteen hundreds there were many sailing ships still in use, not splendid clippers, but everyday working craft, and there were always several moored to the quay, loading or unloading, smelling of tar and wet canvas. They were not pretty, and usually very dirty like their crews; but in my opinion romantic, and when very young I used to ask my father or brother if one was ours, because my mother frequently remarked that I would receive something I desired "when our ship comes in". Later I realised that our ship was only imaginary, but the sight of those dirty brigs gave me longings to board a ship and travel to many foreign parts. These longings were fortunately fulfilled during my adult life.

The magnificent double decker iron High Level bridge spans the River Tyne near the quay, carrying the railroad on top and other traffic below, connecting Newcastle and Gateshead. It is several hundred yards in length – a tiring walk for foot passengers – so before the advent of tram-cars and motor vehicles, horse omnibuses called "brakes" or more usually "flea chariots" were available for those who could afford to pay one halfpenny per trip. On my visits to the town I would be given a round trip as a special economical treat for one penny. These vehicles plied for many years and when the service ended, when motor buses connected the two towns, the last trip was made a special occasion for celebrations.

The twelfth century castle from which the city takes its name stands high above the quayside, and is reached from it by climbing a long steep flight of stone steps named The Dog Leap Stairs. When I was a boy, and for some time afterwards, these steps were bordered by quaint ancient shops and houses, almost slums, a sort of English Casbah, and the business carried on was harness and clog-making. Clogs were often worn by folk doing rough work, and when washing clothes, to raise their feet from dirt and water on the pavements or floors of factories. They were made with thick wooden soles with iron strips, and had uppers of real leather, so such footwear was almost everlasting, though a pair cost only a shilling or two. I loved the smell of leather, and watching cloggers and harness makers plying their trade in open-fronted workshops, and the sight of finished clogs hanging down in strings, and had to be dragged away by my escort. Visits to the Castle were rare because of the admission charge, and I entered it only with a party from school on an educational tour.

"Gannin doon the toon" on Saturday nights was precluded for children of our stratum of society because, I discovered later in my teens, there was much drinking and drunken brawls in the streets. The gutters here and there contained helpless drunks who were picked up by the police and allowed to sleep off their debauch at the police station, or, if their address was known, delivered to their homes by kindly constables.

Provincial folk usually speak of going up to London, Geordies always speak of "gannin doon to London". I was privileged to "gan doon" for the first time at the age of ten. I use the word privilege, as few boys or girls of our class visited London, looking upon that city as an enchanting place something like an Eldorado far, far beyond their reach. My father made annual visits to attend Provision Merchants' conferences and came back regaling us with tales of banquets usually held at the Holborn Hotel, where eight or more courses were served in the Edwardian fashion. As he was such a strict teetotaller he must have missed out on the accompanying wines and spirits provided. He stayed economically with boyhood friends who had been educated with him at The

114

30: The Empire Theatre in Newgate Street, in about 1911: 'perhaps best of all' of the variety theatres in Newcastle before the First World War (see p.124).

Friars Mission School, and had obtained appointments in London. One close friend was a Mr. P- – who had done so well in life that he had become Clerk of Works at Buckingham Palace, and lived in a little villa in its grounds.

The decision of my parents to give me a trip to London was kindly made because I was the only one of the whole family who had not been there, and as the visit would be educational. Father made me promise to write an account of it. I reneged on this promise till writing this book.

My eldest brother, Alec, counted as the clever one of the family, had taken a degree in science at Durham University, specialising in biology and entomology, and had been appointed an assistant lecturer. He must have been a brilliant researcher, because an eminent government scientist suggested he would be a useful person to study the problems of insects, pests and parasites in Nigeria. At that time the parasites inducing malaria had only just been discovered by Professor Ross, and there was still much research on this and other diseases to be done. To discuss the problems, Alec had to make several trips to London, and on the last one before his appointment was confirmed, Father decided to go with him, and I should go also. Money never being plentiful in our family, it was arranged that Father only would travel by train and Alec and I by ship, which was very much cheaper, especially steerage class. Ships of the Tyne and Tees made regular passages between Newcastle and London, the outward and inward runs each occupying about twenty-two hours. Being counted as an infant, my return fare was five shillings, and I think my brother paid one pound for his. We were booked to sail in a well-known very old ship, the S.S. *Highlander*, far past its best, having made the passages between ports in Scotland and London for many years. To me, a very small boy, she looked immense, lying against the quay and towering above it. I have mounted many gangplanks, boarding ships sailing to far off places, but never with so much excitement and anticipation as I did mounting that of S.S. *Highlander*.

A sailor examining tickets at the top of the gangplank, pointed forward and said "Up in the stem for you lads." We went in the direction he had indicated and found a hatchway leading down into the fo'c'sle which consisted of a very cramped triangular space containing twenty bunks in tiers along its sides. There was no

116

panelling so the berths were set against the ribs and iron plates of the ship. There was a long narrow table and wooden forms in the confined space between the rows of bunks, and these were the only furniture provided for steerage passengers.

Alec and I were soon on deck again, after being allotted bunks and storing our luggage on them, to see the ship cast off mooring ropes and begin her voyage down river. She passed close by the famous liner, S.S. *Mauretania*, which had recently been launched from Wallsend shipyard and was being fitted out, then on, passing other yards till we came near the mouth of the Tyne with the towns of North and South Shields on either bank. A passenger leaning over the ship's rail, remarked, using a very common catch-phrase on Tyneside: "Aye aarl togither like the folk o' Shields", which puzzled me as the inhabitants were separated by a broad strip of water, and I never found out the derivation of it until I began writing this book. Years before it was dredged it was possible to ford the river between the two towns during a very low tide.

Alec warned me that soon we would be crossing the bar at the river mouth and the ship would "hike" a little, meaning bob up and down. It did; but the movement was entertaining rather than disturbing. Clear of the bar, the ship turned to starboard for its long run down the coast to the Thames.

Soon, a greasy steward, beating a frying pan, called the steerage passengers to our evening meal. We sat on the forms against the long, bare table in the fo'c'sle, and the steward at one end ladled out food from a large iron pot on to enamel plates, giving generous helpings. I can remember that meal to this day, as it was my first experience of rough eating. It consisted of stewed meat, potatoes and cabbage swimming in greasy gravy, plus bread and margarine and mugs of tea. The passengers, all rough looking types, ate with relish, and waited, expecting pudding to follow; and when it did not arrive, shouted for the next course. The steward replied "Gentlemen, the next course is the reckoning – one shilling and threepence each and ninepence for the boy." There was some grumbling, but the passengers eventually paid up, as the steward stood at the hatchway and would not allow them on deck till they did.

Soon, owing to the sea air, I was feeling sleepy, so Alec tucked me up with blankets on my bunk and I slept, but not for long. I was wakened by feeling my bunk sinking down from me, then lifting me upwards. The steward, grinning, was distributing large washing-up bowls to all the bunks, as the ship was pitching and rolling with a sickening motion, intensified at its stern. The atmosphere in the fo'c'sle was foul, as several of the passengers were smoking strong twist tobacco, whilst playing cards. I immediately threw up, losing my dinner, and lay in misery and some fear as waves crashed against the ship's plates an inch or two from my head, and water crashed on the deck above me till nearly dawn, when the seas were calmer.

Breakfast consisted of finnan haddock boiled in water, not in milk as we had at home, and I could not touch it, but was grateful for a mug of hot, strong, sweet tea. No other meal was offered, and when we entered London River, I forgot my seasickness and munched sandwiches and a piece of bacon-and-egg pie which Mother had provided for the voyage. She never permitted any of her family to travel more than a mile or two without providing provender, in fear lest we died of hunger.

I can remember little of sightseeing on that visit to London, but recollect little incidents which I recounted later to my school friends *ad nauseam* on my return home, till they accused me of "swanking", a word just coming into use. Father and I stayed with our friends in their villa near one of the gates of Buckingham Palace grounds, and I vividly remember being taken round the stables and allowed to sit for a few seconds in one of the state coaches, and playing about in the grounds and eating what Father called the "King's mulberries", and being told, if any important looking lady was about, to make myself scarce, as Queen Alexandra occasionally visited Mrs. P– – and took tea with her.

I remember a long ride, sitting on top of a horse omnibus near the driver, from the Strand to Shepherds Bush, and the journey seeming interminable, and being hypnotised by the rumps of the horses jogging up and down. As a special treat, I was taken for a ride on one of the few motor omnibuses, which were just coming into use, and was the envy of my friends. Strange how tiny incidents stick in childish minds – and I shall never forget staring at the barefooted scarlet-coated crossing-sweepers operating near Piccadilly Circus, and my father presenting one with a penny for his trouble.

I looked ahead with trepidation to our return voyage, fearing more seasickness, but the weather was fine, the sea calm, and we had some amusing fellow passengers. We sailed during an evening, before the pubs had closed, so there was no one drunk, but some of them were merry and in good form for a party on deck. One had an accordion, and another a fiddle, and both played the instruments so well that Alec spotted they were professional music hall artistes. Starting with popular songs in which everybody joined, the concert developed into a series of individual turns, when one chap, slightly tipsy, did an expert clog dance. This was followed by a conjuror doing sleight of hand with coins and cards, then a tenor soloist, and a comedian reciting comic verse. Unfortunately, the party developed into a drinking bout, and I was sent to my bunk by brother Alec, where I slept soundly throughout the night and woke to eat a hearty breakfast.

The steerage passengers were segregated on a small part of the ship's deck, so I could not explore the rest of the ship, and became bored and a little homesick, which led me to inscribing my first unsolicited piece of writing on a slip of paper – "At sea on S.S. Stephen Furniss – bored to death; yours truly, Basil Peacock". I then placed the paper in an empty lemonade bottle, corked it, and threw it into the North Sea. I have often wondered if it reached a shore, was found, and if so what the finder thought about it.

When Alec and I reached home, Mother welcomed us as though we had voyaged to the ends of the earth and back again. She was very concerned that Alec had been appointed as Government Entomologist to Nigeria, and had already begun equipping himself with tropical kit in London. She was even more alarmed when he produced a revolver which the authorities had advised him to carry when touring in the jungle. Naturally, this firearm interested and intrigued me and I determined to travel to exotic far-off lands when I was old enough. Only eight years later I revisited the villa in the Palace grounds, and I was carrying a pistol, as I was then an infantry subaltern on my way to the Western Front. Thankfully, I got my wish, and know now that tropic lands cast a spell over the majority of visitors to them – the minority loathe them – and that once you have been in the jungle, the jungle will always call you back.

In Alec's case, it nearly killed him, because Nigeria and its neighbouring countries were known quite rightly as "the White Man's Grave" in 1910. He survived eighteen months, and came home rotten with malaria and had to be dosed with quinine for months, and forbidden to return to the tropics.

CHAPTER TWELVE

Growing Up

When I was 13 years old, I was thought old enough to participate in more adult amusements, and it was Alec who introduced me to theatre going. He was already an addicted play-goer, and gradually persuaded my parents that theatres were not necessarily dens of infamy. Father must have been nearly fifty years of age before he saw his first play, a Shakespearian drama starring Forbes Robertson, and discovered he had been missing a great deal by writing about Shakespeare but omitting to see his plays acted on the stage. He soon became a regular theatre-goer if he thought the productions were serious and educational. However, he did take Mother and me to see the "Christy Minstrels", then at their height of popularity and touring Europe, when they gave a show at the Empire Music Hall in Newcastle. I was a little too young to appreciate and remember all the entertainment, but recall that the performers were what most people called "blackamoors" then, and sang jolly songs such as "Swanee River" and "Camptown Races". Most of their jokes were incomprehensible to me, and I was very puzzled why one of the company being addressed as Mr. Interlocuter caused great amusement.

However, I remember details of my first visit to a real theatre vividly. I was twelve years old when Alec decided to take me and his sisters to a performance of Peter Pan at the Theatre Royal, which was, and still is, one of the finest theatres in England. He could only afford seats in the gallery and gave us full instructions on how to behave in the scramble for the best seats, because gallery-goers were rarely orderly queue-formers. As we waited in the crowd outside the ticket office, and the stairs going aloft, he said: "As soon as I have bought the tickets at sixpence each, you and I will sprint up those stairs as quick as we can, leaving your sisters to follow, and we will try to bag front seats". I still remember that scamper up what appeared to be unending stone steps, and the first sight of rows of benches mounting steeply one behind the other almost to the roof. They appeared very precipitous, and when climbing down them to the front row, I was fearful I should trip and fall over the edge into what Alec called the pit stalls. I was disappointed that we were not entirely placed at the very front, as there was a guard rail and three rows of seats in front of it. Alex explained that they were called the "amphitheatre" and cost ninepence each, which was beyond his purse for five of us. I was also a little disappointed as we settled in our places that the stage seemed so far away and there was a stiff curtain in front of it, with advertisements for butchers' and drapers' shops painted on it. However, after what seemed an interminable wait, this was whisked up out of sight, and a beautiful velvet curtain with gold tassels was exposed; musicians popped up in front below, and tootled on instruments, then played a lively tune as footlights came on. The curtain parted and I saw my first stage scenery and set, a child's bedroom with a large window at the back and a large dog kennel at the side. I was entranced as I still am, at the rise of a curtain at any live stage performance. I have never seen another performance of *Peter Pan* on the stage, and no film or television production of that play has given me more enjoyment. Unfortunately, we were seated so high up in the theatre that we glimpsed what we were not supposed to see. When Peter and the children flew away out of the window, the stage lights reflected from the flying wires so that the illusion of flying was somewhat spoiled, and when the pirates were thrown over the side of the pirate ship we could see that they landed on mattresses and cushions and a stage hand threw up a handful of rice to indicate splashes of water. I thought that Captain Hook was the star of the performance, as I was very disappointed that the person taking the part of Peter was a girl. I also thought it a little silly and embarrassing to be asked to clap our hands to indicate we believed in fairies, and thus save Tinkerbell's life, because at my age I had given up believing in ordinary fairies, though I was pretty sure there were leprechauns in Ireland.

I returned home a fervent theatre-going addict and having a somewhat retentive memory, I was able to quote pieces of dialogue, and nearly drove Mother frantic by repeating *ad nauseam* Captain Hook's words: "That is where the canker g-gnaws."

My next visit to the Theatre Royal was to see a performance of the musical comedy *The Arcadians*, this time in the amphitheatre seats as Alec was in funds. I was entranced by the scenery, the costumes, and the first entrance of the hero, played by Dan Rolyat, who landed in Arcadia from a mock aeroplane; and by a real race horse brought on to the stage in the second act. The lugubrious jockey, Peter Dooday, made me laugh uproariously, and again I drove Mother and the family frantic by repeatedly singing about the house his song: "I've gotta motta – always merry and bright" in mournful tones, till forcibly ordered to desist.

A few years later, in 1913, I was privileged to see that famous stage pair, Jack Hulbert and Cicely Courtneidge, then playing minor parts of a valet and a maid in the musical comedy *The Cinema Star*, a piece imported from Germany, which deserved more success than it had, because anything of German origin was dropped when the Kaiser's War began, but I still remember one of the principal songs "Auf dem nacht" – "In the night, in the night, when the moon's at its height", etc.

Another very entertaining musical comedy was entitled *Yes, Uncle*, which was very tuneful, and I would suggest that some television producer should do some research and revive it, as I believe it never has been revived. As one of the scenes depicted an artist's studio, with half-naked girls posing as models, it could be an immediate success in these permissive times. I still remember some of the words of a song sung by a trio of principal male actors, all with love trouble.

> "We men ought to combine, ought to combine, fall into line,
> All pull together like birds of a feather,
> And stick through rain or through shine,
> Each for all and all for each,
> United we stand, divided we fall;
> And if you don't mind a suggestion of mine
> I think we ought to combine – yes – yes,
> We certainly ought to combine."

All the Peacock brood were Gilbert and Sullivan fans, and I was weaned on the Savoy Operas, but there my education in music ended, and maybe this is because I love tunes and have no ear for grand compositions except the bits that are tuneful to me. I became such a devotee of the D'Oyly Carte repertoire, that once when I was a young soldier receiving three shillings and sixpence a week,

122

I spent three shillings, at sixpence a time, for a gallery seat at the Lyceum Theatre, Edinburgh, during one week.

With the development of moving pictures, small picture halls were beginning to open for business, and I was allowed to attend performances unaccompanied by an adult. One opened in Worley Street, which runs or used to run off Westgate Road. I think it had been an old chapel or mission hall, with a small gallery. Admission prices were one penny on the ground floor and twopence in the gallery, so were within reach of my purse because my pocket money was twopence a week. The performances were attended mainly by children, and occasionally by intoxicated men from nearby pubs when these closed after the midday sessions. I can only remember one film I saw. It was called *A Child's Dream*. The story was very simple and, as usual, sad and sentimental. A poor ragged child with drunken parents was wandering the streets as its home was a place of fear. Worn out, the child, who turned out to be a girl, fell asleep in a gutter with her head resting against the curb. A drunken man sitting near me was overcome with emotion at the girl's plight, particularly because she had done some heavy acting business before finally succumbing in the gutter, and he kept repeating "A child's dead, a child's dead – poor little bugger", and he wept alcoholic tears over me before falling asleep himself. The film proceeded as the child dreamt a handsome, bearded man came by, took pity on her, picked her up in his arms and took her off to his own home where she was treated with every kindness and eventually adopted. The audience knew it was a dream, as her real body was still lying in the gutter. Then the film stopped, and an announcement made on the screen: "There will be an interval while we change the spool". When the film began to run again, a handsome man did come along, mimed his grief at the sight of the girl, picked her up and took her home where she was treated with every kindness and eventually adopted. The film ended with a shot of the little girl, now no longer worn and sad, but dressed in fine clothes and bowling a hoop, smiling and laughing. My drunken neighbour woke up and exclaimed "The child's not dead – the child's not dead – the little bugger's aal reet now", and shed more alcoholic but joyful tears as he applauded the performance. The Worley Street picture hall eventually had to close down, mainly because of new regulations regarding precautions against fire when showing films, and was a sad loss to children who looked forward to spending their pocket money and seeing moving pictures for one penny.

When a few years older, with a little more pocket money, I used to attend performances at the Palace Theatre in Percy Street, which specialised in melodramas, such as *Maria Martin, or Murder in The Red Barn, Sweeney Todd, the Demon Barber of Fleet Street, The Face at the Window, East Lynne,* and many others now almost forgotten.

The entertainment was not only on the stage, but also provided by the audience, which was often composed of rather unsavoury and drunken types who came to cheer, heckle or boo the players, especially the villains. I recall sitting in the gallery beside two very drunken ratings off a warship, come to see a performance of a jingoistic piece about the British navy, the name of which I forget. They made derogatory remarks about life in the Royal Navy as depicted on the stage, but their patriotism was aroused by the bravery of a sub-lieutenant rescuing the heroine from the dastardly clutches of foreign pirates. One, leaning far over the gallery rail, shouted for all to hear: "Hooray for the R.N. orficers – they may be all snotty buggers, but them's the lads, they're aal snotty but spunky fellies as weel".

I look back with pleasure, and feel fortunate that I, when a lad, saw many of the old music hall artistes in the flesh, before they died and became legendary. The old time music hall of Victorian times, with its chairman, and with drink served in the auditorium, had faded out, but variety theatres were flourishing before the First World War. There were at least three in Newcastle, the Grand in Byker, the Tyne in Westgate Road, and, perhaps best of all, the Empire in Newgate Street, which I patronised when I could afford to. Most of the artists had been on the boards since their childhood, and when I saw them were getting past their best, but still were good troupers, with voices of brass which could reach the topmost gallery seats without the help of artificial aids. There were no female impersonators or 'drag artists' then, except the dames in pantomine; but male impersonators, such as Hetty King, were popular, and kept their female outlines when doing their turns. Hetty invariably finished her turn dressed as a guardsman, singing a patriotic song. Marie Lloyd made no pretence at being anything else but a female busting out all over. She was a mistress of innuendo and her patter was what is now termed 'blue'. Albert Whelan, who hardly altered his turn for decades, was an unusual artiste who could entertain audiences for twenty minutes by doing very little, slowly, with only a trifle of patter, a song, and one or two jokes. I can remember the substance of his act. He entered the stage slowly, from the O.P. side, immaculately dressed in evening clothes, with opera hat and red silk lined cloak and silver topped stick, whistling his signature tune, a German lieder 'Lustige Bruder'. He was reputed to be the first artiste to invent a signature tune, and he continued to whistle it as he removed his gloves, finger by finger, placing them in his hat when he removed it. He then carefully placed his cane on a chair, removed his cloak, folded it and placed it on top. The whole of the procedure occupied about six minutes, while the audience sat spell-bound, waiting for him to do something funny; but he was not a comic, and just expertly whistled something akin to 'Tales from the Vienna Woods'. After this, he remarked that he wished to tell a story of the three trees, which was approximately as follows:

> Once in a desert was a small pond and three trees there, there and there. Then three gazelles came to drink at the little pond with the three trees there, there and there, but then came a lion to drink at the little pond and the three little gazelles scampered away over the desert in fear. The lion roared, then began to drink and when he had finished, bounded away across the desert leaving the little pond deserted and the three trees there, there and there.

The rest of his act was taken up with him putting on his cloak, hat and gloves, very slowly, and whistling his signature tune while making his exit. It was extraordinary how he could hold an audience while telling his story, and halfway through they started joining in with "there, there and there".

One of my favourites was Maudie Edwards, a sort of subdued edition of Marie Lloyd, with a good voice and clever patter with innuendoes, about husbands, lovers and forward girls. She used to caper about the stage holding up her skirts to show a leg up to the knee, and sang about how she was trapped into a sad marriage on a windy day because "If the wind had only blown the other way, I might have been a single girl today".

Unless they are septuagenarians or older, there can be few persons left who saw the turns of 'Little Tich', 'The White-eyed Kaffir' (Chirgwin), or 'The Chocolate Coloured Coon' (G. H.

Elliot), though their songs are still sung by imitators. Little Tich was an expert dancer and comedian whose gimmick was a pair of boots with absurd, long toes. The Chocolate Coloured Coon was an expert dancer and singer whose most famous song is still revived: 'By the light of the silvery moon'. The White-eyed Kaffir, called that because of a white patch over his left eye, did his turn in a calm, intimate manner now copied by several television artists. He sat on a low stool on a bare stage and played a fiddle, and sang sentimental songs in a pure, high tenor voice. The most popular were 'The poor blind boy', which brought tears to the more sentimental in the audience, and 'My Fiddle is my sweetheart'. Towards the end of his act, he changed to a one-stringed fiddle held upright on his knee, and in a serio-comic manner sang:

An old beer bottle came over the sea,
An old beer bottle came onto me,
And in it was a message, and these words were thereupon,
Whoever finds this bottle – finds the beer all gone.

Most of these artists were enormously popular in their time, but died or faded away during or soon after the First World War, and I have sometimes wondered if their turns would be received so rapturously in this modern age when audiences are so sophisticated and brought up on 'the box'. Nevertheless, it is pleasing to note that the television show *The Good Old Days* was one of the most popular ones, and the Leeds Empire still flourishes, resurrecting the old acts and music hall personalities.

Sadly, those variety theatres I attended as a boy, the Grand, Byker, the Palace (known as the Dirty Alice) and the Empire, once one of the finest theatres in Europe, are now razed to the ground and replaced by modern glass and concrete buildings which provide no entertainment for boys.

31: A class at Rutherford College in 1910 (form IVa in room 21). Here the author spent 'several . . . formative years . . . acquiring some higher education' (see chapter 13).

CHAPTER THIRTEEN

College Boy

I spent several of my formative years at Rutherford College, Newcastle, acquiring some higher education. After my time there, the name was changed to Rutherford Grammar School, and later it became a co-educational establishment similar to a rather superior comprehensive school.

It was founded in 1877, and owes its existence to a great evangelist and physician, Dr. John Hunter Rutherford, who was born in Jedburgh in 1839 and who spent many years of his life raising the educational and religious standards of the people of Tyneside. In the mid-nineteenth century, it was difficult for children of poor parents to receive even elementary education, and the good doctor, assisted by members of the Church, founded an elementary school in Bath Lane which gained a great reputation. He soon realised the necessity for secondary education, and the need to provide opportunities for boys from all classes of society to qualify for professions such as engineering, chemistry, architecture, civil and naval, and others where services were badly needed in the mines, factories, and other industries, now that Britain had entered the industrial age. In my time, though the arts and humanities were included in the curricula, they took second place to science.

When I first entered the college, receiving general education in the lowest forms, I made the mistake of being too earnest a scholar, and after two terms was unwisely promoted to an upper form two grades higher, where my supposed brilliancy was immediately dimmed, and I missed some valuable instruction which I have regretted ever since. Later, without reference to me or my parents, I was placed in what was later termed the Science stream, where I almost drowned, as I never had any wish or talent to become a scientist.

Literature and the classics were taught in some seclusion by a gentle master who loved his work and taught ably. He was the only member of the staff who detected in me a liking for literature, after hearing me read a passage from Shakespeare when in a junior form. He told me to stay behind when the rest of his class were dismissed, and queried: "You appear to understand and have real feeling for the words of the Bard, am I correct in thinking so?" Being ashamed that I might be called a swot by my class mates if I replied yes, I said "No, sir". He shook his head sadly, remarking, "Pity, I thought I had discovered a lad who might make a classical scholar – but I fear you are similar to an actor who can act and declaim his part with apparent emotion, then retire to the wings and drink a pint of porter, glad that his job is done". So, because of my foolish remark I lost the opportunity to be rescued from scientific studies which I loathed, and when I was introduced to higher mathematics, I gave up trying to learn, and finished my secondary education at the bottom of the sixth form. I often wonder what my future would have been if Tommy Moles, the classical master, had shaped it.

Despite my poor showing in class, I sat for the Durham University Matriculation Examination and to my surprise and that of my teachers, was given a pass. One rather acid and sarcastic master asked me if this result was true, and when I affirmed that it was, he announced to the whole class that it was the most extraordinary result he had heard during the whole of his teaching career. I still feel sour about this remark to this day.

The college then was a place of cramming, and to quote a remark of an old Scots dominie, "Pupils were dragged up the slopes of Parnassus by the scruff of their necks." Games and sport were hardly looked upon as part of our education, and I feel that when we were despatched to the Town Moor to play football, or some desultory cricket, the main object was for us to take some clean air into our lungs. The College Building was situated in a slummy part of Newcastle, almost adjacent to a tannery and a brewery, which smelt abominably. Remarking on this to an ex-master, years later, he added: "and some of the boys also." On the afternoons devoted to football, the pupils had to carry goal posts, marker flags, etc., half a mile to the moor if the school janitor was not available to transport them in a hand cart. It was some years after I started college that players turned out in proper football kit, in jerseys and shorts, and I cannot remember anyone dressed correctly in white for cricket.

During the last two years of my attendance the college had a small field, fully a mile away, where senior teams played games and held running races. The one young enthusiastic master introduced us to rugby football and spent a great deal of time training those boys interested. I was no good at soccer, but took to rugger with pleasure. Being small, but robust, I played scrum-half for the school team and continued the game after school days were ended by joining the now famous and successful Gosforth Rugby Club.

Possibly because I played for the rugby team, Mr. Gaunt, our headmaster, appointed me a prefect, but I cannot remember contributing to the discipline of the juniors, as so many of them were much taller and heftier than I was at that time. Mr. Gaunt was a fine Christian gentleman who had the presence and qualities of an able headmaster. He was a splendid speaker, and when he read from the scriptures or made speeches even the disorderly or rowdy lads listened with attention. I remember him making two appropriate and laudable speeches with deep emotion, one when he announced the loss of the S.S. Titanic with 1500 passengers in 1912, and another in the same year when describing the deaths of Captain Scott and his companions and the heroism of Captain Oates who tried to save them by leaving their tent in a blizzard after they had reached the South Pole. Mr. Gaunt was held in some awe by his staff and scholars but was a kindly and considerate man. I record this because of his compassion when I returned home on leave from the Western Front in 1917 and visited the college. He greeted me in his study with moist eyes, exclaiming, "Oh, Basil, my boy, it is so good to see you – thank God you are safe and uninjured – so many of my old boys I shall not see again; the numbers of fatal casualties have been appalling".

During the later years at college, the world, and to some extent social life, began to change rapidly. Most far-off parts of the globe had been discovered by explorers, and North and South Poles reached by valiant men on foot without mechanical aids. Communications, by radio and with bigger and better ships were shortening the passages over the seas, and motor cars, no longer sources of wonder, were appearing in the streets. A few years before, with other boys, I had run a mile after the first car we had seen passing our church. A year after M. Bleriot had flown across the Channel in his monoplane, a similar aircraft made a tour of England, and I saw it flying high across the Town Moor to land at Gosforth Park, and what most people had thought of as legendary flying machines were now a reality.

Looking back over the years to the last of my boyhood days, I still marvel that the mode of life of my family and millions of others changed so rapidly in a matter of weeks during 1914, because there were few signs that such a transformation was to take place. The habits and activities in most families in Newcastle had been constant during several decades, except for improved methods of transport, and the introduction of gas and electricity for heating, lighting and cooking. Families and relatives had been close-knit even after members had married and left the homes of their parents. Except for sailors, soldiers, and skilled engineers, few folk had travelled extensively and even a trip to London was a much discussed event. Then, within a short few weeks after the 4th of August, when war against Germany was declared, tens of thousands of men left their homes for life in the armed services and travelled to places and countries which had been known to them only in geography books.

In 1914, the broadcasting of news by radio to people's homes had not begun, and newspapers were not so widely distributed and read as at present. Not every household had one delivered daily, and copies were usually bought from newspaper sellers in the streets, so news of events, especially foreign affairs, took some time to reach many of the population. Boys seldom read newspapers, but could not help noticing the headlines on placards outside stationers' shops. I regularly walked with three companions two miles to college, and one morning we read that an Austrian Archduke had been assassinated in some strange place with an unpronounceable name in Europe, but thought little about it, till, after a few days, the placards announced that several countries were preparing to go to war. To boys, this was more exciting than alarming and it was more exciting still when I saw two workmen pasting-up a large bill on the notice board of a nearby church. It was coloured red, white, and blue, and headed "General Mobilisation". On reading it, I found it had nothing to do with the church, but it stated that all reservists of the armed forces and members of the Territorial Army must immediately report to their depots and drill halls. At the foot of the bill in large print were the words "God save the King".

Within a few days the humdrum lives of most families changed as unusual events occurred. One of the first was when a battalion of soldiers, headed by their band, marched past our house in the suburb of Wingrove where we were now living, and took up billets in the nearby elementary school. The unit was the 4th Territorial Battalion, East Yorkshire Regiment, and on first sight of them, and listening to the military music, I determined to be a soldier as soon as possible.

Rutherford College was closed for the summer holidays, and by the time it opened again, hostilities on the Continent had begun. Our masters tried to explain to us why Great Britain had declared war on Germany, but most of the senior boys cared little for the *casus belli* but were anxious to leave school and take part in the war. Several of the most senior boys who were junior members of the Territorials or the Naval Volunteer Reserve had already left school and joined their units. Our French master, M. Maubousin, had departed to join his regiment of Chasseurs in France, and soon sent a number of photographs of himself in uniform for distribution to the staff and prefects. I have one still, showing him in the old-fashioned uniform of *poilus*, a kepi head-dress, a long blue overcoat, and baggy red trousers with a sword by his side. Sadly, only a short time after receiving the photographs, Mr Gaunt announced at morning assembly that our respected master had been killed in battle during the early days of the fighting in France. Many of us thoughtless lads had believed war a great lark, and this first fatal casualty began to alter our opinions.

There were posters all over the town calling for recruits to the Territorial Army, and to Lord Kitchener's New Army; and men and boys of all ages, some falsifying their ages, besieged the recruiting centres to enlist. With few exceptions, the older boys were in a fervent mood to leave school and join the armed services, and when it was known that those aged eighteen who had passed matriculation could be accepted in the Durham University Officers Training Corps, many joined, and surprisingly soon blossomed into second lieutenants and came in their uniforms to say good-bye to the college. I was too young to join, but enlisted in an organisation called the Junior Training League and received a red, white and blue cord to wear round the shoulder seam of my jacket, of which I was intensely proud.

The three lads with whom I walked to school were a little older than I, and were some of the first admitted to the Officers' Training

Corps. They were commissioned and tragically all lost their lives in action before they reached adult age, as did the majority of the college rugby team, of which, to my knowledge, only four survived the war. On the college War Memorial are the names of 152 old boys who died in battle during the 1914–18 war, nearly all of whom were scholars during my time at Rutherford.

I left college in 1915, and the only traces now of my presence there for several years are some humorous articles I wrote for the college magazine, copies of which I still possess. I note that I first got into print in 1914. I then became an unwilling pupil teacher in an elementary school for a few months, and spent as much time as I could serving with the University O.T.C.

CHAPTER FOURTEEN

Goodbye to Boyish Days

At the beginning of 1914, the situation report on the Peacock family (to use a military term) was as follows: Father, Mother and their six children were living in the west end of Newcastle, and the most important difference from our home in Cheltenham Terrace was that our house was lit with electricity and we had a gas cooker. Alec was a lecturer at Armstrong College, Durham University; Jim was a school-master and thinking of getting married; Edith was helping Father in his business; Eleanor had opened a china shop; Jennie was an infant school teacher; and I was at college, and recently promoted to long trousers.

By the end of that year both Alec and Jim had enlisted in the Army, though both having served in the OTC should have waited to be offered commissions, which they later received. I was very jealous of them in uniform, and being a nuisance wanting to join them. At the beginning of 1916, it was known that conscription was soon to be introduced. As I was still too young to be commissioned, but wanted to be a volunteer like my brothers, I went to Fenham Barracks, falsified my age, stating I was nineteen though I was actually seventeen and enlisted in the Royal Fusiliers.

My parents were most distressed, Mother saying, "I have given two sons, is not that enough?" and Father remarking, "Well, you have made your own bed, and now you must lie on it." Secretly, he was proud to declare to other parents "All my sons are serving in the Army and all are volunteers."

I left my home for Oxford, where my unit was billeted, accompanied by a school mate who had also falsified his age, and sadly was killed on the Somme.

Thus my boyhood ended, as within a few hours I had to become a man and soldier. Despite some difficulties and dangers I have never regretted entering the profession of arms. My subsequent adventures in far-off places and two World Wars are recounted in another book of mine, *Tinker's Mufti*, the memoirs of a part-time soldier (published by Seeley Service 1973).

Envoi

I have now entered what my father used to quote as 'the quiet eventide of life'. Looking back over the years I realise how fortunate I was to be the son of worthy Christian parents who sacrificed themselves to ensure that their children had the best education they could afford. I have also been fortunate that the family remained close-knit, and that there was none of that antipathy between members which occurs sometimes and separates brothers and sisters.

My life has been full of interesting experiences and adventures which I had wished for since a boy, and despite some mistakes and inconsiderate conduct in my salad days I have few regrets. Like most of my generation, I am not jealous of those of younger generations living in a more affluent society, but also in a much disturbed and polluted world.

I thought I had no regrets till recently I read the quotation –

"Golden lads and girls all must
As chimney sweepers come to dust."

and I began to realise that my generation of boys had no time to become golden lads because the First World War precluded us from enjoying ourselves with no cares or responsibilities, and many came to dust long before they should.

THE PEACOCK FAMILY TREE from c.1810

Three brothers named PEACOCK all born in Newcastle upon Tyne
before the Battle of Waterloo, 1815:

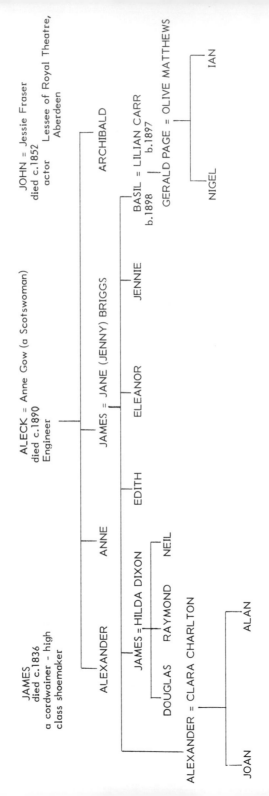

JAMES
died c.1836
a cordwainer - high
class shoemaker

ALECK = Anne Gow (a Scotswoman)
died c.1890
Engineer

JOHN = Jessie Fraser
died c.1852   Lessee of Royal Theatre,
actor   Aberdeen

ALEXANDER

ANNE

JAMES = JANE (JENNY) BRIGGS

EDITH

ELEANOR

JENNIE

ARCHIBALD

JAMES = HILDA DIXON

BASIL = LILIAN CARR
b.1898   b.1897

GERALD PAGE = OLIVE MATTHEWS

DOUGLAS   RAYMOND   NEIL

NIGEL   IAN

ALEXANDER = CLARA CHARLTON

JOAN   ALAN

The Peacock and Briggs clans were very prolific and at the early part of the twentieth century
I (Basil) had over forty cousins and many uncles and aunts, but, to my knowledge, I now have
(c.1980) only one cousin, Dora Spires, née Dora Briggs.

Pedigree

Tracing family descent is now a popular pastime, but most researchers, members of ordinary families, having no historical background, have difficulty discovering facts about ancestors who lived and died before *circa* 1836 when the Central Registry Office was established. Before then, all records of births, marriages and deaths were kept in parish churches by the incumbents, some efficient and some casual. Thus it is essential for a researcher to know the parish in which a forbear lived and died, and so is fortunate if he has various old documents and letters which have been retained for decades in family archives.

Fortunately, my father retained some documents which enable me to record these facts.

Three brothers, James, John, and Alexander Peacock were born in Newcastle in the first decade of the nineteenth century. James, the eldest, died before the second half of the century and I have in my possession his will which was made in 1836. It is written on parchment in copperplate handwriting. I also have the form of probate issued from the office of 'James Baker, Clerk, Master of Arts, Vicar Principal of The Right Reverend Father in God EDWARD by divine providence Lord Bishop of Durham'. (In those days the Ecclesiastical Authorities dealt with such matters).

James was described as a cordwainer (a shoemaker using Spanish leather) and he left all he possessed, which was under £200 to 'his dear wife Ann'. His early death *circa* 1844, and his funeral were tenderly described in a letter written by Alexander to John who then lived in Aberdeen. The letter is too long to quote in this book but the following extract indicates that James was a popular and loved member of the community.

"It was an affectionate sight to see all his Brother Foresters at the funeral – they sang at the door and at the grave; there never was such a Foresters funeral in Newcastle nor won't be for some time to be . . . there was not one that know James but said there was never a finer lad ever walked Newcastle streets."

John, the next brother, was something of a rover and possibly looked upon as not quite respectable because he was an actor and in those days actors were still regarded by many people as rogues and vagabonds. His stage name was John Pollock, and he had some success as a player in the provinces and elsewhere, because his name is recorded in the records of the Pollock's museum. I have an old playbill dated 6th June, 1847, advertising his benefit night at Barnsley Theatre Royal, when he played Petruchio in *The Taming of the Shrew*. I also have some of his letters describing his travels with a company of players, and their poverty and hardships which were analogous to those of the Crummles acting family described by Charles Dickens in *Nicholas Nickleby*. At one time in his career he was taken seriously ill in the Isle of Man, almost penniless and without adequate clothing, and I have a pathetic letter he wrote to his brother, Alexander, asking for help. He was rescued by a lady friend of his, Miss Jessie Frazer, the lessee of the Theatre Royal, Aberdeen, who nursed him back to health, took him back to Aberdeen, and married him; and he spent the remaining years of his life in Scotland.

Alexander, the youngest of the brothers, was our grandfather, who lived till a ripe old age, spending the last few years of his life in our home, and died during the last decade of the nineteenth century. He could recall hearing the first news of the victory of Waterloo reaching Newcastle when he was a lad. He died before I was born, but my brothers remember him well. He married a Miss Gow and had three sons and a daughter, my father and my uncles Alexander and Archibald. Annie, the daughter, died of a decline early in life, and I remember that hanging on a wall in our house, was a memorial tablet to her consisting of some verses which began "Dear Annie thow hast passed away, our home is very sad today."

This is all I know of my pedigree, but my grandsons, now in their twenties, when they reach my age should be able to trace family descent back for over two hundred and fifty years.